WHERE'S THE MATH?

Books, Games, & Routines to Spark Children's Thinking

Mary Hynes-Berry & Laura Grandau

National Association for the Education of Young Children
Washington, DC

National Association for the
Education of Young Children
1313 L Street NW, Suite 500
Washington, DC 20005-4101
202-232-8777 • 800-424-2460
NAEYC.org

NAEYC Books

Senior Director, Publishing and Professional Learning
Susan Friedman

Editor in Chief
Kathy Charner

Senior Editor
Holly Bohart

Editor
Rossella Procopio

Senior Creative Design Manager
Henrique J. Siblesz

Senior Creative Design Specialist
Charity Coleman

Senior Creative Design Specialist
Gillian Frank

Publishing Business Operations Manager
Francine Markowitz

Through its publications program, the National
Association for the Education of Young Children
(NAEYC) provides a forum for discussion of
major issues and ideas in the early childhood
field, with the hope of provoking thought
and promoting professional growth. The
views expressed or implied in this book are
not necessarily those of the Association.

Permissions

NAEYC accepts requests for limited use of our copyrighted
material. For permission to reprint, adapt, translate, or otherwise
reuse and repurpose content from this publication, review
our guidelines at NAEYC.org/resources/permissions.

Photo Credits

Photo illustrations by NAEYC: 6, 32, 35, 40, 44, 64, 76, and 101

Courtesy of the authors: 71

Copyright © Erin Donn: 110

Copyright © Vera Wiest: 24

Copyright © Getty Images: cover, iv, vi, 4, 6, 12, 13, 16, 17, 18, 21,
23, 26, 28, 34, 35, 36, 38, 40, 42, 44, 50, 51, 58, 61, 62, 64, 66,
68, 76, 78, 82, 86, 90, 91, 98, 99, 103, 105, 106, and 112

Where's the Math? Books, Games, and Routines to Spark Children's Thinking.

Copyright © 2019 by the National Association for the Education of Young
Children. All rights reserved. Printed in the United States of America.

Library of Congress Control Number: 2019935618

ISBN: 978-1-938113-51-2

Item 1140

CONTENTS

v   Preface

1   Introduction

MATCHING & SORTING

10   Chapter One
**How Are These the Same?
How Are These Different?**

14   Not Quite the Same

18   Resorting to (Re-)Sorting

22   Sorting with Shoes

26   Oh, the Weather Outside!

PATTERNS

30   Chapter Two
What Comes Next?

36   Pattern Detectives

40   Stairstep Story Patterns

44   Cycles as Patterns

48   And . . . Action!

NUMBER SENSE

52   Chapter Three
**How Many Do We Have,
Need, or Want?**

56   Some Frogs Here,
Some Frogs There

60   A Treat to Eat

64   Counting By Feet

68   Counting in My World

MEASURING

72   Chapter Four
How Big Is It?

76   Building with Blocks

80   Finding the Right Fit

84   Bigger This Way,
Bigger That Way

88   The Letter Club

SPATIAL RELATIONSHIPS

92   Chapter Five
Where Is It?

96   Obstacle Course Adventures

100   Shaping Up a Quilt

104   Shape Scavenger Hunt

108   Build-It Challenge

113   **Final Thoughts**

114   **Glossary**

116   **Book List**

118   **References**

119   **Resources**

120   **Acknowledgments**

121   **About the Authors**

PREFACE

This book grew from our extensive knowledge about and passion for two topics—storytelling and math. Our many years of collective experience watching and helping children discover the magic of math informed the activities you will find in these pages.

Mary has been doing oral storytelling in classrooms for more than 40 years, and she is always finding new ways to give beloved tales a mathematical twist. Laura loves combining children's own story ideas with math talk to help children (and adults!) see, hear, and play with math concepts. We never fail to be intrigued and delighted by children's creativity and problem solving as they act out stories or engage in extending activities.

We hope early childhood educators will find this book full of ideas and inspiration to incorporate mathematizing magic into their classrooms. The strategies and suggestions for exploring specific math ideas and skills have come from our personal work as well as more than a decade of work with our associates at Erikson Institute's Early Math Collaborative, reaching thousands of young children in Chicago and around the world.

While we believe in these ideas, we are also committed to the principle that activities alone cannot bring math to life in the minds of young children. Effective teaching and learning depend on teachers making intentional instructional decisions about which experiences will best address well-focused learning goals—and then engaging children with thought-provoking questions and conversations that build on their interests, discoveries, strengths, and needs. Tapping into children's natural curiosity and wonder is the key to making math concepts fun and meaningful.

And children's faces looking up
Holding wonder like a cup.
—Sara Teasdale, "Barter"

INTRODUCTION

Becoming a lifelong learner and problem solver is rooted in wonder and curiosity. As an early childhood educator, you have a unique opportunity to nurture these traits in children by listening to the many questions they ask about the world, helping them explore what they notice in meaningful ways, and engaging them in rich conversations that spark even more discoveries, deeper understanding, and new wonderings!

Many of the things children naturally wonder about are bursting with math, as are the stories they read, the games they play, their day-to-day routines, and the real-life problems they face. You just have to look to find it: "The chart says it's my turn next, right?," "Will my new school be bigger than this school?," "Zak, we need two more long blocks for the wall. Can we use four medium ones instead?" Think about a book the children in your class love hearing read aloud, whether it's a fairytale, a classic children's book, or a new picture book. Is there a problem the character or characters must solve? Now look a little harder—how can you find the math in the problem situation?

When you have an eye for seeing the math all around us, you can guide children in finding it for themselves.

Building Math Minds

You can build on children's natural curiosity and observations to help them grow into confident problem solvers and investigators of math concepts. To do so, it's helpful to understand a few basic principles about how to make math both meaningful and enjoyable in early childhood—and beyond.

Learning Math Is Grounded in Conceptual Understanding

We are all born with the ability to do math, but like walking and talking, it takes a lot of practice! Unlike walking and talking, however, math is much more than a skill—it is a conceptual understanding that develops over time. You don't need to know the mechanics of how your brain and nervous system and muscles work together to walk across the room, but to do math, you do need to understand how numbers can be used to find out "how many" objects are in a collection or why it's important to specify what kind of "big" you're talking about before you can determine or compare an object's size.

When using words like . . .			To say things like . . .	You are talking about . . .	
bigger	loudest	tiny	"Do you want two more apple slices?"	compare and contrast relationships	magnitude
colder	more	wide			measurement
lots	saltier		"The puppy is smaller than the big dog."		quantity
alike	the same		"TJ chose the same kind of van as you, but his is different because it's red and yours is white."	making sets sorting	
different	similar				
beneath	near	pointy	"I think the ball rolled under the table."	geometric attributes (shapes and lines)	
down	next to	round			
far away	over	under		spatial relationships	

Engaging children in math talk while exploring stories, events, and interests that matter to them is an effective way to help them make sense of essential math concepts. No matter what a child's home language or culture is, mathematical concepts are already built into everyday speech and communication from early on. Some common examples are shown in the figure above.

Of course, depending on the context, words like those in the figure could be part of conversations about many other math concepts besides the examples named. Math concepts connect, overlap, and build on one another; they do not exist as isolated ideas.

Young children's use and understanding of mathematical language evolves over time. The more they hear math words and see them demonstrated in the context of their everyday experiences, the better developed their mathematical thinking skills become. For example, a toddler might call every animal with four legs he sees *dog*.

As important people in the child's life respond to his use of the word, including pointing out differences, the child processes this information and matches it to categories that already exist in his mind. Over time, he learns that while both a dog and a horse have four legs, a horse is something different from a dog. In the same way, children's understanding of mathematical concepts also becomes more precise. While a young child might be able to recite the words for the numbers 1 through 10, this does not mean that she understands that the word *ten* means there is a quantity of exactly 10 things. Teaching number words *and* number concepts together is essential to scaffolding understanding and open-ended thinking.

Be intentional about using language that brings out the math as you talk, interact, and play with children. As they experience mathematical ideas in many different contexts and gain an understanding of basic math language, children are ready to explore increasingly more complex mathematical concepts.

Math Is Everywhere

Many early childhood experts agree that mathematizing is a critical starting point to help children understand and be interested in math. *Mathematizing* means seeing math in daily life and using mathematical language and concepts to frame, analyze, and explore situations. You are mathematizing when you

- Engage children in talking about their ride on the bus this morning: "How many people were on the bus with you? How long did it take you to get to school this morning?"

- Ask a child to tell you more about the drawing she made of her home: "My bedroom is upstairs. It has two beds, one for me and one for my sister."

- Help children resolve real-life problems and conflicts: "Joey, I hear you saying it is not fair that you have two cars when Taahira has four. What could you both do about this? . . . Okay, Joey's idea is that he plays with all six cars for five minutes, and then Taahira plays with all six for five minutes. . . . You don't like that idea, Taahira? What if you line up all the cars together and each choose one at a time so you each have an equal number? Or maybe it would be more fun for you both to play with all six cars together?"

You can also develop intentional learning experiences and lesson plans around mathematizing. What are the children interested in? What kinds of things do you hear them talking about? What's going on in their families and communities? A mathematical inquiry is most meaningful for children when it is integrated with something they are already familiar with and interested in. This is true for everyone across all areas of learning—it's easier for us to grasp new ideas and ways of doing things when they are tied to things we already know. Because they are such an important element of every child's life, stories, games, and routines are powerful entry points to create and introduce high-quality mathematical experiences—even if they don't initially appear to be math focused.

> The children in Mr. Van's kindergarten class are doing an author study on Mo Willems. Although this is a literacy study, Mr. Van ties in math experiences to the children's interests. The reading center has a big collection of Willems's books, and the children are discussing how to organize them all. With Mr. Van's guidance, they decide to sort them by series: one group for all the books about Knuffle Bunny; one for Pigeon books; another group for books about Elephant and Piggie; and one for Elephant and Piggie Like Reading! books.

On a poster board, Garrett and Anika draw a chart that displays how many books are in each series set. Another display on the wall shows the results of a survey the children conducted as a whole group with Mr. Van to find out which books are everyone's favorites, how many children have the same favorite book, and which book is the biggest favorite.

Sakura, Gerald, and Liam decide to act out *We Are Growing*, an Elephant and Piggie Like Reading! book by Laurie Keller. Mr. Van observes them as they work out how many children are needed to play all the characters (blades of grass!) and how they will act out growing taller. The next day, Liam brings in a photo of the growth chart his parents have used to track his height since he was a baby. Excitedly, other children begin sharing and comparing the growth charts that their own families have at home. Mr. Van is delighted by all the math learning that is coming out of what appeared to be a literacy study!

Helpful Websites

Here are a few online resources that are full of ideas for how you can mathematize learning experiences in your classroom.

Development and Research in Early Math Education (DREME) Network: https://dreme.stanford.edu

Erikson Institute's Early Math Collaborative: https://earlymath.erikson.edu

Illuminations, by the National Council of Teachers of Mathematics (NCTM): https://illuminations.nctm.org

Math Is More than Just Getting the Right Answer—It's About Questions and Thinking

Math is so much more interesting and complex than rote counting and labeling, flash cards, or number problems on a worksheet. It is a useful, meaning-making way of thinking that is steeped in *logical-mathematical thinking*. This means using reasoning skills to

- Identify the problem or what you want to know: "What size wagon do I need to hold all of my blocks? Where should I put the wagon so the blocks are easy to get out and put away in the block center?"

- Find a solution by analyzing the situation and using cause-and-effect thinking to understand the relationships among objects, actions, or ideas: "How many blocks do I have? Does the wagon I need fit in the block center right now? How can I rearrange the room so I can bring the wagon closer?"

It is more important that children learn to be mathematical thinkers than it is that they can recite the right answer to a question or problem. Even in cases where there is a single correct answer, it is important to understand that there are different ways to arrive at that solution. Emphasize the process more than the solution, and cultivate this mindset in the children. This emphasis on process, thinking, and reasoning also ties in with the mathematical practices outlined by the Common Core State Standards (see "Standards

Standards for Mathematical Practice

Children develop the problem-solving skills and processes they need to succeed when you provide them with math experiences that focus on the following mathematical practices outlined by the Common Core State Standards for Mathematics (NGA & CCSSO 2010):

1. Make sense of problems and persevere in solving them.
2. Reason abstractly and quantitatively.
3. Construct viable arguments and critique the reasoning of others.
4. Model with mathematics.
5. Use appropriate tools strategically.
6. Attend to precision.
7. Look for and make use of structure.
8. Look for and express regularity in repeated reasoning.

for Mathematical Practice" on this page. When you value children's thinking and reasoning, you encourage them to think through situations themselves, try out a variety of strategies, and communicate their ideas and what they've learned. These are skills that apply to every part of their lives.

Young children are very concrete thinkers, and they need many hands-on experiences and opportunities to talk about what they're doing before they can generalize the mathematical concepts they are learning. For example, it is likely to take some time for a child be able to transfer the skill of counting animals in a picture to counting out and handing someone exactly three stuffed animals from a box. It will take even longer to understand the idea that a quantity can be put together (composed) and broken apart (decomposed) in many different ways. A group of six animals might be made up of six snails; two dogs and four cats; three foxes and three rabbits; or one turtle and five fish.

If we think of understanding as a lightbulb, the path to switching it on is different for each individual. As children work together, ask questions, and share their ideas, they hear and consider things they haven't thought of before and develop vital problem-solving skills like collaboration, communication, brainstorming, and flexible thinking. When you facilitate this process by using what each child knows and ask open-ended questions that inspire deeper thinking, children are better able to make the meaningful connections between what they know and what they want to know until that lightbulb switches on. The questions you ask and the conversations you start scaffold children's learning and encourage children to consider their thinking from a whole new angle, which helps children develop abstract thinking skills. As you find opportunities to invite children to explore and make discoveries through the questions you ask them, the more questions budding mathematicians will come up with themselves!

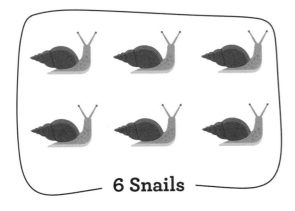

6 Snails

2 Dogs & 4 Cats

3 Foxes & 3 Rabbits

1 Turtle & 5 Fish

Math Is for Everyone

All children bring to the classroom their individual *funds of knowledge*—the body of knowledge, skills, and experiences they've built through interactions with their families and communities. This means children will see things differently and will use different methods to make sense of what is happening as they explore math. For example, a child who speaks both English and Chinese might name a quantity of 12 objects as "ten two." A teacher who has made efforts to learn more about this child's home language might realize that unlike English, Chinese has a regular number word system. That is to say, while the English language has unique words to name numbers larger than 10, the Chinese language combines the words for 1 through 10 to create larger number words. In English, the number word for 12 is "twelve" while in Chinese it is *shi er*, which literally translates to "ten two" (Rasmussen et al. 2006). With this understanding, the teacher can work to bridge the child's knowledge between both languages. Scenarios like this are why it is critical to respect and build on each child's funds of knowledge. Accepting only certain answers as right and dismissing the ways other children represent their understanding is wrong. Not only is this not what math is about, it's counterproductive.

One approach to making math learning more inclusive and equitable is to use rich storybooks as a springboard. Exploring math by examining problem situations in a story or in real life makes math approachable and invites children to engage with the problem and come up with a solution. Books that are most likely to spark mathematical thinking share several characteristics:

- A strong story line or theme
- A problem that children can think about logically
- Engaging text and illustrations
- Something new or interesting to think about every time you read it
- An invitation to explore and play with ideas in a meaningful way

Time and again, play has proven to be one of the most effective ways to build on and reinforce children's learning. Play invites children to be actively involved in problem solving not only cognitively but also physically, socially, and emotionally. Consider which question would get children more engaged in finding the solution to the problem: "How many dogs were chasing the Gingerbread Man?" or "How many of you need to pretend to be the dogs chasing the Gingerbread Man?" The first question is just looking for a set answer, while the second gets children emotionally invested because it is linked to a real-world situation: "I want to be a dog! One . . . two . . . three . . . three of us can be dogs!"

About the Book

This book focuses on five questions that children wonder about and ways you can guide children to investigate and understand these questions. Because this is a book about math, the chapters explore how to bring out the logical-mathematical thinking at the heart of these questions. The order of the chapters reflects the way children's mathematical thinking develops, from less complex to more complex and from concrete to abstract.

How Are These the Same? How Are These Different? (Matching and Sorting)

By the time they are in preschool, many children know how to put away books and toys, organize a collection of treasures, and create a birthday wish list. Everyday actions like these become mathematical when you intentionally guide children to focus on

- Identifying and naming key attributes of objects

- Using precise, or specific, language

- Making rules about what attributes all items in a set must share

- Comparing, contrasting, and ordering objects by size, type, color, or quantity

What Comes Next? (Patterns)

Children, like all humans, are always trying to understand, establish, or change patterns and structure. Young children need many repeated, guided experiences to develop the ability to identify and describe the patterns all around them, from the sequence of daily classroom routines to the motions of a finger play to the repeated words in a story. Identifying the structure of patterns allows them to predict what will come next—and children love to be proven right! As their thinking develops further, they become aware of more complex patterns that are rooted in math; for example, birthdays follow a plus-one rule and the number of monkeys jumping on the bed follows a minus-one rule.

How Many Do We Have, Need, or Want? (Number Sense)

From a young age, before they know and can use number words, children know when they want *more* or *less* of something. This is the beginning of understanding the mathematical concept of quantity. It can take a while before children are precise about how *many* more or fewer of something they need or want. They need plenty of time, experiences, and practice to explore counting and number operations before they can estimate or come up with an exact answer to the question of *how many?*

How Big Is It? (Measuring)

Young children tend to believe that bigger is always better. You can guide them toward using more logical thinking around the concept of size. To figure out how big something is means exploring more specific questions about *what kind* of big we are thinking about. Do we want to know how tall the boat is (height)? How long it is (length)? How wide it is (width)? How old it is (age)? How heavy it is (weight)? How many people it can hold (capacity)? Understanding the question of how big something is also means offering children lots of measuring experiences that have them explore

- Understanding when a general sense of size is good enough (estimation) and when a more precise measurement is needed

- Using direct and indirect comparisons

- Using standard and nonstandard units of measurement

Where Is It? (Spatial Relationships)

Most children have had the experience of trying to find someone (a friend on the playground, a family member in the house) or something (a toy in their bedroom, a book in the reading center). To find what they are looking for, they might remember that the person or thing is located in relation to someone or something else (their friend is playing by the swings or their stuffed penguin is in a basket on the shelf). With repeated experiences like these, they come to realize that following or giving directions requires logical thinking and precise use of language. For example, being told that a favorite toy is *somewhere* isn't helpful, but it only takes a minute to find it when told "I saw it under the yellow chair in the back of the room."

Each chapter of this book introduces mathematical problem situations that explore one of these questions. To make the investigation of each of these questions meaningful for young children, they are embedded in children's books, games, and routines and include lots of opportunities for conversation. These mathematical explorations are most appropriate for children in preschool and kindergarten, and they are flexible enough that slight adjustments can be made to make them more or less complex as needed for diverse learners. Each chapter also includes a list of math concepts supported by the activities in it.

The practical activities and ideas in this book link *math* with *questions* and *wonder*. This mindset may be quite different from your own experiences in school, where it might have been drilled into you that right answers and speed are more important than understanding. By embedding investigations in stories and real-life problem situations for children and engaging them in intentional, thoughtful conversations about math, you are laying the critical groundwork for later mathematics.

As with any resource book, begin at the place that makes sense for the children you teach. You know your curriculum and the strengths and needs of the children in your classroom best, so it's up to you to choose and tailor experiences that are a good fit for them. Reflect on what children learn from an experience, what they express interest in, and how you can build on their growing understanding to extend the concepts. If some children seem to need more time to explore a concept, repeat an activity or change it up.

As you explore these stories and activities with the children, we hope that all of you will experience the wonder that is math!

Chapter One

MATCHING & SORTING

HOW ARE THESE THE SAME? HOW ARE THESE DIFFERENT?

Math Concepts Explored in this Chapter

- Attribute
- Binary sorting
- Comparing

- Comparing and ordering sets
- Exact matching

- Matching
- Multiple set sorting
- Open sort

- Set
- Single attribute sorting
- Sorting

Almost from the moment they are born, babies can sense in a very general way that the things they feel and the world around them can be the same or different—warm or cold; full tummy or empty; sleepy or wide awake (Gopnik, Meltzoff, & Kuhl 2001). As they grow into toddlers, they begin to compare and contrast various qualities, or *attributes*, that people, places, or objects may share. At this age, children are especially aware of attributes that they can discover through their senses, like size, color, smell, taste, sound, and texture. They also use more and more specific words to explain what they like and what they don't, but they still depend on making sounds, facial expressions, and gestures to communicate that while red is their favorite color, they don't like red tomato juice or that scratchy red sweater. By the time they enter preschool, many young children begin to think logically about the ways attributes can be used to organize objects.

Exploring Matching and Sorting

The preschool class at Rocky Glen School returns from an excursion with their first grade buddies. They collected pinecones, seeds, twigs, and other natural treasures outdoors, and now they are sorting their finds into bins.

Six-year-old Tina is helping 3-year-old Aza use the word and picture labels on the bins to match the objects she has picked up. "This is the same!" Aza announces as she holds a pinecone up to the photo on one of the bins and then drops it into the bin. "We can't put the seeds here 'cause they don't match," she tells Tina, who nods and helps Aza find the bin labeled *seeds*.

Another pair of buddies, 4-year-old Timon and 7-year-old Jaz, had decided to collect only rocks while they were outside. The rocks in their basket range from small, smooth pebbles to large, chunky stones. Jaz grabs a few containers

that do not have labels and says, "We have to figure out how to sort our rocks. There are lots of ways they are the same and different." Timon takes one container and says, "Can I do just my favorites, the little shiny ones we found in the creek?" "Go for it," Jaz laughs. He works on the other rocks, clustering the medium-size rocks into a pile together and tossing the biggest rocks into a pail. As he works, Jaz examines the rocks more carefully and exclaims, "Timon, our rocks are same and different in some really cool ways. Some are just brown or black, but I'm seeing some that are kind of striped and others like this one, all speckled black and gray." Timon looks over and then finds one of his smaller ones, declaring, "This is speckledy too!"

Ms. Priti, the preschool teacher, comes over to see what is so exciting. As both boys pull out more examples, she smiles and says, "What superstar observers you two are! You could

How Are These the Same? How Are These Different?

11

put the ones that are speckled in one container and then decide what other categories you want to use. What do you think?" The boys enthusiastically agree and set to work. Because Jaz is so intrigued by the many different types of rocks he is seeing, Ms. Priti makes sure to point out the rock books she put on display in the science learning center in preparation for this activity.

Young children's understanding of the rules that guide matching and sorting, or dividing and organizing a group of objects into sets by shared characteristics, follows an established developmental trajectory (Early Math Collaborative 2014).

Exact matching, or recognizing and identifying objects that are completely alike, is the earliest stage. In the vignette above, when Aza sees that the pinecone she is holding looks the same as the one on the photo label on the bin, she understands that items with the same exact attributes can be matched.

Single attribute sorting expands on matching. Timon and Jaz begin sorting their rock collection by focusing on size. Jaz, who is older, can see that it makes sense to break the large collection into three categories of size: small, medium, and large. Very often, younger children will do single attribute sorting using color because determining the difference between red, blue, and green objects is much more straightforward than judging differences in size, which can be more relative.

Binary sorting is closely related to single attribute sorting—a collection of objects is divided into two distinct sets, one set *with* a specific attribute and one set *without* that specific attribute. Essentially, this is what Timon does when he takes all the small, shiny rocks from the collection and leaves the others for Jaz to deal with.

Multiple set sorting calls for focusing on several different attributes and creating increasingly complex categories based on those attributes. Timon is happy to follow Jaz's lead in deciding which rocks are a solid color, speckled, or striped, but Jaz sees that he could make one set of rocks that are large and have different colors in them and another set of rocks that are large, are a single color, and have a rough texture.

Comparing and ordering sets means observing and analyzing different sets of objects to compare them using specifically mathematical attributes: amount (quantity) or size (magnitude). By the time children are a year old, they have a strong natural instinct to look at groups of objects and wonder "Which has the most?" or "Which is the biggest?" (Sarnecka 2016).

You can turn just about any classroom activity into a mathematical experience through conversations. For example, ask the child who enjoys playing with toy vehicles to tell you how rescue vehicles are the same as and different from delivery vans. Not only will she enjoy sharing her expertise, explaining these similarities and differences will help consolidate her understanding and lead to new discoveries and learning.

Using Open Sorts to Promote Mathematical Thinking

As children have more and more experiences with sorting objects as well as gathering and interpreting information, they develop a more complex understanding of the various ways they can organize collections. Eventually, they discover that a collection of objects can be sorted in many different ways based on the attribute or attributes they choose to look at. It is important to provide children with a lot of opportunities to do open sorts, where they can sort a random group of items any way they want. This encourages logical thinking. When children are organizing and sorting objects, encourage them to explain the rule they used. You will be surprised and delighted with how deep and flexible children's thinking can get when they are engaged.

When sorting experiences are linked to children's everyday lives, they make meaningful connections and grasp the math concepts more readily than when they work with commercial objects that have specific, limited ways to be sorted. They are more engaged and likely to have excited conversations about what makes the sets the same or different. When you provide materials for children to sort, look for items that invite interesting investigations, like these:

- Bottle tops
- Buttons
- Paper
- Old keys
- Natural objects, like rocks and twigs
- Rubber bands
- Yarn

You might ask families or local businesses to donate items or visit thrift stores or your local reusable resource center. A number of websites offer information on finding nearby reusable resource centers, including www.reuseresources.org.

How Are These the Same? How Are These Different?

13

NOT QUITE THE SAME

Inspired by *A Mother for Choco* / Keiko Kasza

The Story

Choco wants a mother, so he sets off to find one. He asks Mrs. Giraffe, Mrs. Penguin, and Mrs. Walrus if they are his mother because he notices each looks like him in one way. Each animal then points out that she also looks very different from Choco in another important way. Choco is very sad that he can't find an animal who looks just like him to be his mother, but when he comes across Mrs. Bear, she shows him that love has nothing to do with what you look like on the outside.

Consider the Math Concept

Both the text and the illustrations in the story compare and contrast two different animals, first by focusing on one physical attribute they both share and then by looking at another physical attribute that makes them different. To develop children's logical-mathematical thinking, keep this exploration and the activity a conversation rather than a question-and-answer session with closed-ended questions.

Letting the children study each page of the story closely, make discoveries, and express their ideas will build their observation skills and support their understanding that having one attribute in common does not mean two objects or two creatures are exactly alike. Digging deeper into how even a shared attribute can be similar without being *exactly* the same can also help children learn to express their ideas more precisely.

PLAN

Materials

■ Large easel, dry erase board, or chart paper
■ Markers

This activity can work in small or whole group settings. Young preschoolers will get the most out of the activity when you observe and support them in groups of three or four children. On the easel, dry erase board, or chart paper, draw a chart like the one on page 15 large enough for all the children to see and to allow room for more than one response.

Where's the Math?

Explore and Investigate Together

After sharing the story together, ask the children why Choco thought Mrs. Giraffe, Mrs. Penguin, or Mrs. Walrus could be his mother. What did he notice about himself and about them? Why do they think that when he first saw Mrs. Bear, he thought she couldn't be his mother?

In a way that is visible to all of the children, display a page from the book that shows Choco and one of the animals he thinks might be his mother. Ask the children to carefully study the illustrations and to share any ways they notice Choco and that animal are the same and are different. They may note attributes that are specifically mentioned in the story as well as some that are not. As the children offer observations, write down their responses in the chart.

Talk About the Math

Offer specific feedback about how the children are thinking, and use open-ended questions and prompts that help children figure out how things are related.

- You remembered that Choco and Mrs. Penguin both have wings. Are there any other ways you think the two of them are alike? How?
- Can you think of any other animals that are similar to Choco? How are they alike?
- Kai, that was very observant of you to notice that Choco does not have teeth while Mrs. Walrus has two very long teeth!

	Mrs. Giraffe	Mrs. Penguin	Mrs. Walrus	Mrs. Bear
Choco is the *same* as this animal because they both . . .				
Choco is *different* from this animal because he . . .				

How Are These the Same? How Are These Different?

15

Individualize the Activity

- Some children will find it helpful to focus on just Choco and one other animal at a time. Use a blank piece of paper to cover the names of the other animals until they are ready to move to the next one. In some cases, it might work best to extend the activity over several days.

- Add animals that aren't featured in the story to the chart. Place photos of these new animals (from reference books or found online) where the children can observe them. Once they have had time to study the photos, ask the children if they noticed anything similar to or different from Choco.

- Children who have mastered this concept might enjoy making their own book about an animal that is similar to a few creatures in some ways and different from those creatures in other ways.

- Using what the children have learned about how animals are the same and different, facilitate a game of 20 Questions.

More Books

Home / Carson Ellis

Is Your Mama a Llama? / Deborah Guarino, illus. Steven Kellogg

Same, Same but Different / Jenny Sue Kostecki-Shaw

How Are These the Same? How Are These Different?

17

RESORTING TO (RE-)SORTING

Inspired by *Five Creatures* / Emily Jenkins, illus. Tomek Bogacki

The Story

A girl talks about the five different creatures who live in her house: her, her mom, her dad, and their two cats. As she describes how they are the same as and different from each other, she groups the five of them together in many different ways!

Consider the Math Concept

All kinds of attributes are used to show how the five creatures in the story can be sorted into different groupings, depending on what the girl chooses to focus on. When she looks at hair color, she, her mom, and one cat are together in one group because they all have orange hair, while her dad and the other cat are in another group because they both have gray hair. But when the girl considers size, she is now in a group with both cats because all three of them are short, while her mom and dad make up another group because they are tall.

Children love the activity that follows this story because it is all about them, but it also is a great way to double-dip math and literacy. Precisely naming and describing the attributes used in open sorts is an effective way to help children build a robust vocabulary.

Where's the Math?

Materials

- Masking tape, rope, or Hula-Hoops
- Costumes and accessories from the dramatic play area (optional)

This activity works best in whole group settings. Using masking tape, create two circles on the floor large enough for a few children at a time to stand in. Alternately, if there are fewer children or if you aren't able to place tape on your classroom floor, use rope or hoops. If the children wear uniforms or if you simply want to add a larger variety of attributes for the children to consider, invite them to select something they can wear from the dramatic play area (a hat, a scarf, a cape) before beginning the sorting activity.

Explore and Investigate Together

After reading the story, ask the children to name some of the things the girl in the story noticed about herself, her parents, and their cats. Why do they think sometimes the girl is in a group with one or both of her parents and sometimes she's in a group with one or both cats? How about when she's in a group all by herself?

Divide the children into two groups, one group of five to six children to be sorted and the remaining children as another group to act as sorting checkers. The sorting checker group will need to carefully observe the children who are being sorted because you are going to ask the checkers if the other children have sorted themselves correctly. Explain that together, you are going to sort them into two groups based on things they have in common. Begin by modeling this activity with a binary sort: "I see that some of the children in our group to be sorted are wearing something red and some aren't. If you are wearing something red, step inside the blue circle. If you are not wearing

anything red, go stand in the green circle. Now, sorting checkers, it's time for you to do your job—is everyone in the right circle?"

Call on children from the sorting checker group to identify the red item each child standing in the blue circle is wearing. Help the children count and discuss how many children are in each group. With the children still in their same roles, model at least one more binary sort using another visible attribute, such as children who are wearing sandals and those who are not. As the sorting checkers confirm that the sorted children are standing in the right circles, guide them through comments and questions to discuss how even though the same children were being sorted, the groupings changed.

Once the children seem to grasp how the activity works, invite a new group of children to be sorted and ask the sorting checkers to look at what the children are wearing and make suggestions for how the group could be sorted.

How Are These the Same? How Are These Different?

19

Talk About the Math

Use comments and open-ended questions that invite the children to think about and discuss the attributes being used for the activity. Help them realize that while there aren't necessarily right or wrong answers, the group has to agree on a precise definition for each attribute in order for the sorting to be accurate.

- Brielle, you are saying you should be in the red group because you have red stripes on your sweater, but everyone else in the red group is wearing an item that is solid red. What do the rest of us think? Should the rule for being part of this group be that the item must be *completely* red or does it just need to have *some* red?

- I can see you are really looking at our group carefully, Antain! That was a great idea to sort by children who are wearing a belt and those who aren't.

- Each of the three times we've sorted the children in this group, we split them into two smaller groups. Can anyone think of tricky sort that would put everyone in just one group?

- **Ms. Moreno:** How many children are standing in the red hoop?
  Tory: Three and umm, they all got boots on.
  Ms. Moreno: Excellent observation, Tory! They do all have boots on. Does anyone notice something about the other group?
  Miguel: I know! *(Pauses. Ms. Moreno smiles, waiting patiently.)* Shoes! Those two got shoes.
  Ms. Moreno: They do, don't they! So what can we call that group?
  Miguel, Tory, and the other children: The Shoe Group!
  Tory: And the other guys are the Boot Group!

Individualize the Activity

- If some children find this activity too difficult, work up to people sorting by giving them plenty of opportunities to sort a small collection of items that are obviously the same and different in a variety of ways.

- Once children are comfortable with making binary sorts, make this activity more challenging by increasing the number of the children being sorted or adding a third circle for another attribute.

- Provide children with five to 10 related items, like a collection of stuffed animals or different food items, and ask them to create two sets using a rule they choose. Take photos of the sets children create and have the children either dictate or write their thinking for how they sorted the collection. The photos and the children's words can make for great documentation displays.

More Books

"A Lost Button" from *Frog and Toad Are Friends* / Arnold Lobel

Sam Sorts / Marthe Jocelyn

Sort It Out! / Barbara Mariconda, illus. Sherry Rogers

Other Resources

To see how this activity was carried out with a preschool class of dual language learners, visit https://earlymath.erikson.edu/people-sort-elementary-school-math-games.

For an excellent discussion about sorting and suggestions for more open sort activities, visit https://playingwithlearning.weebly.com/classifying-and-sorting.html.

How Are These the Same? How Are These Different?

21

SORTING WITH SHOES

Inspired by *Shoes, Shoes, Shoes* / Ann Morris

The Story

Wooden sandals, open-toed mules, soccer cleats—there are so many different kinds of shoes! With this book, explore the shoes people from different cultures around the world wear while walking in the snow, working, playing, and more.

Consider the Math Concept

This book takes the idea that a collection can be sorted in many different ways to a new level of abstract thinking. It shows how sorting can go far beyond comparing items based on a single attribute like color, style, or type of material. Objects, like shoes, can be described and classified with increasing precision, moving from very broad to very specific categories. Those sets can then be compared and ordered. Using a graph gives young children whose number sense is still developing a clear visual of how the quantity in each set compares.

Coming up with names for groups based on attributes might seem obvious to adults, but children who are still developing the ability to think abstractly and use language to express these more complex ideas need back-and-forth conversations that include repetition. It's important for them to feel comfortable struggling for the right words, so wait patiently and encourage their responses warmly.

PLAN

Materials

- Plain shower curtain liner
- Masking tape or markers
- Camera

This activity works best with groups of 10 to 15 children. Use masking tape or markers to create a grid (typically, a layout that's four by five or five by five works nicely) on the shower curtain. This will serve as a *realia graph*, a form of 3-D bar graph that uses real-life objects.

Explore and Investigate Together

Give children plenty of time to explore and have conversations about *Shoes, Shoes, Shoes*, including making connections to their own shoes. Then pose this problem to the children: "What if we were going to make a book about the shoes we are wearing today? What might be a good way to sort and organize them?"

Gather the children in a large circle and ask everyone to place one of their shoes in the middle. Once the children have had a few minutes to make observations about the shoes, ask them for ideas about how the collection could be sorted into groups. At first, children are likely to come up with an assortment of unrelated categories that overlap, such as sneakers, shoes with Velcro straps, and purple shoes. Help them settle on three or four exclusive categories to use, such as type of shoe (sneakers, dress shoes, sandals); type of fastener (laces, Velcro, buckle); or color. At the same time, keep in mind that children are generally more engaged when you let them come up with the sorting categories than when you tell them how to sort the shoes. Even young preschoolers will come up with very thoughtful, creative open sorts.

Bring out the realia graph and explain that it will help everyone compare how many shoes are in each category. If this is the first time the children have used a realia graph, take the time to describe how it works:

- Each column begins at the line (axis) drawn along the bottom of the grid.
- Only one shoe can be placed in each square on the grid.
- Fill in each grid square beginning at the axis and working up. Point out that skipping a square makes it difficult to compare the number of items in each column.

Label a column for each of the categories you will be using. Have each child place her own shoe in a square on the grid, but be prepared to guide her in placing it in the correct column and row. When the graph is complete, give the children plenty of time to study it and discuss the data. Use your camera to take a picture that can be used to revisit the graph and continue or extend the activity another day.

Talk About the Math

Prompt children to think about what questions—and answers—the data suggests. Plan some questions ahead of time, but also follow the children's lead.

- Since most of us have our uniform shoes on, almost all of the shoes are brown. Instead of looking at color, what might be another way to create groups?
- What should we do about shoes that both light up and have laces?
- The column of sneakers is much taller than the column of boots. What do you think that means?

Use questions and conversations about the data to go beyond identifying which type of shoe is most common to more interesting questions about *whys* and *whens*, such as these:

- Why do you think so many children are wearing boots today?
- Arturo just suggested that we could put the high-top gym shoes into a separate group—what do others think?
- What if we did this activity when it was hot and sunny? What kind of shoes might we see that no one is wearing today?

More Books

Bread, Bread, Bread / Ann Morris, illus. Ken Heyman

Sorting at the Market / Tracey Steffora

What We Wear: Dressing Up Around the World / Maya Ajmera, Elise Hofer Derstine, and Cynthia Pon

Individualize the Activity

- Younger children will benefit from stretching out this activity over several days. Explore other books that feature shoes, such as *Whose Shoes? A Shoe for Every Job*, by Stephen R. Swinburne, or *Those Shoes*, by Maribeth Boelts, illustrated by Noah Z. Jones. Take time to look through the photos or illustrations that show several pairs of shoes and talk about how they are the same and different. Use these discussions to help children focus on categories that seem especially important to them to use for the realia graph during the activity.
- Have each group of children wearing the same category of shoe gather and take a photo of their feet. Each group can write or dictate a description of the way their shoes are all the same and create a display or classroom book.
- Invite children who are comfortable with the idea that there are many ways to sort a collection to come up with tricky sorts that use two or even three attributes to create a set (shoes that are black *and* have a buckle).

Other Resources

To see how this activity was carried out with a preschool class, visit https://earlymath.erikson.edu/shoe-graph-3-5-year-old-childrens-education-programs-and-activities.

A related activity can be found in the *Young Children* article "Playful Math Instruction in the Context of Standards and Accountability," by Deborah Stipek (Vol. 72, No. 3, July 2017).

How Are These the Same? How Are These Different?

25

OH, THE WEATHER OUTSIDE!

The Routine

Weather is a popular topic for children and adults alike—it influences what we wear, how we travel, what we can or can't do that day, and so much more! Breathe new life into your classroom's weather chart routine by collecting information and comparing and contrasting what changes in the weather mean for everyone on a day-to-day level and how weather changes over time.

Consider the Math Concept

When you connect weather to the way it affects things children have a stake in, they see why collecting information (data) like temperature is important. What can sometimes be a rote routine of data collection then turns into a meaningful conversation that will keep the children thinking and problem solving. With repeated opportunities to engage in activities like this, children develop a deeper understanding of other big ideas related to data—for example, it's useful to compare and contrast data to determine what will happen, and collecting and analyzing data is how we discover answers to more complicated questions. Over time, it is likely that children will begin to check weather reports on television, online, or through mobile apps.

In places where the weather doesn't change as often or drastically, help the children identify the more indirect or different kinds of impacts weather has on their life. For example, as they go from the hot outdoors to indoors where there is air conditioning, there might be adjustments children still need to make. You might also consider partnering with a program or adopting a sister city based in a part of the world with a very different climate and compare the weather conditions with your own city.

Where's the Math?

Materials

- Large easel, dry erase board, or chart paper
- Markers
- Reusable weather symbols
- Outdoor thermometer

This activity works best in whole group settings. Early in the school year, create a weather chart that has space to feature each day of the school week. Each day should have enough space to include

- One to two weather symbols
- A place to record the temperature
- A "Weather and Us" section with plenty of space to note children's observations of how the weather influences their day

Explore and Investigate Together

Explore with the children what we mean when we talk about weather. We can *see* what the weather conditions are, but what other senses can we use to describe it? What does it feel like when it's sunny or windy? Can you smell rain? What does it smell like? Why would we want to know what the weather is going to be before we get dressed? Before we go outside?

Each day, invite the children to describe the outdoor temperature—what the weather feels like (hot, pleasant, sticky, freezing, cool)—and what the weather conditions are like (windy, rainy, foggy, cloudy, sunny, snowy). Have them select one or two weather symbols that they think best represent the day. You might have the children take turns in the role of weather person (or meteorologist, for an extra important title!) to record the answers everyone agrees to. Help the meteorologist read the temperature on the thermometer and record it on the weather chart.

For the "Weather and Us" section of the chart, prompt and guide the children to talk about how the weather affected what they have done and will do today, what they wore today, and other observations, including their thoughts on how the weather is the same or different from the day before. At the end of each week, discuss how the weather was the same or different over the week and what the effects on the children were. Keep each week of the month posted where children can see it. At the end of the month, facilitate a longer discussion in which children explain and explore the discoveries they have made as they gather and describe data about the weather.

How Are These the Same? How Are These Different?

27

Talk About the Math

Develop open-ended questions that help children organize and express their thinking. Your conversation prompts should also be tailored to reflect a particular day or the needs and interests of individual children.

- Ty chose the windy and cloudy symbols for today's weather. What do the rest of you think about these choices?

- Yesterday we used the sunny symbol because it was sunny in the morning, but then it suddenly began to rain in the afternoon, remember? How can we show that on our weather chart?

- What do you notice about this month's weather? How did the number of sunny days compare with those that weren't sunny? How would we count the day that was sunny in the morning and rainy in the afternoon?

Individualize the Activity

- Provide sentence frames (Today it felt _____. It is _____, so I wore _____.) and word walls as clear visual supports so children can make connections between all the data being collected and analyzed.

- If there are children in your class who speak a home language other than English, work with their families or use online translation resources to label the days of the week on the weather chart and the words to describe weather conditions in their home language(s).

- Some children may not wish to be the center of attention as meteorologist. Come up with other ways they might participate in the routine, such as working with a partner where one acts as researcher gathering data and the other presents these findings to the group.

- Explore more sophisticated terms for weather conditions with children, like *blustery, hazy,* or *sweltering.* Ask them to come up with new weather descriptions. Maybe they have sometimes felt like their skin is damp when it's humid or have seen raindrops falling while it is sunny. What symbols and words could they use to represent that experience?

Related Books

Come On, Rain! / Karen Hesse, illus. Jon J. Muth

Sun / Sam Usher

Types of Precipitation / Nadia Higgins, illus. Sara Infante

How Are These the Same? How Are These Different?

29

Chapter Two

PATTERNS

WHAT COMES NEXT?

Math Concepts Explored in this Chapter

- Attribute
- Copying patterns
- Creating patterns
- Extending patterns
- Growing pattern
- Pattern
- Recognizing patterns
- Repeating pattern
- Repetition
- Sequence
- Structure
- Translating patterns

Patterns are sequences in which several objects, events, or attributes follow a recognizable order or progression in a predictable way. They are at the core of everything around us, and the human brain instinctively looks for patterns to help make sense of what is happening and to predict what will happen next. As children have many opportunities to explore patterns, they gradually become aware that patterns follow rules and that understanding these rules means they can continue or even change patterns to meet their needs and wants. These are skills that require logical thinking and that everyone uses, from artists and inventors to computer scientists and mathematicians! Here we discuss two of the most common types of patterns explored in early childhood classrooms: repeating patterns and growing patterns.

Exploring Repeating Patterns

Ms. Mendez teaches kindergartners who are 5 and 6 years old. One day, she overhears Ginny say to another child, "To say a pattern, you just have to repeat—like red, blue, red, blue, red, blue." Ms. Mendez is happy that Ginny is able to recognize and copy a pattern with a basic repeating sequence, but this conversation also makes her realize that it's time to go beyond labeling patterns to scaffolding the children's thinking about how patterns work and the rules they follow.

The following day, Ms. Mendez invites six children to help her demonstrate a game where the object is to figure out the rule for a pattern. She guides them to stand in a specific order, then addresses the rest of the class. "Today I have made a pattern based on one thing about everyone standing up. Everyone who's sitting, your job is to figure out what rule I used to make the pattern. Study everyone carefully, and then let me know what you think my rule is." It takes a few

guesses before Xander excitedly announces, "I know! You used their shirts—Orin has a striped shirt and Domenica has a solid shirt; then Eli's is striped and Bri's is solid; and stripes again on Chandler's and solid for Klaus's." Ms. Mendez smiles. "Wonderful observation skills, Xander! Now, can anyone who is sitting join in to keep the pattern going? What kind of shirt needs to come next, stripes or solid?" Ginny jumps up, pointing to her striped top, and says, "I can! I'll be the next stripe. And Tito can stand next to me because his T-shirt is all brown!"

During group time the following week, Ms. Mendez leads the children in a game of Pass the Pattern. She starts off by snapping once and clapping three times. The children watch her and then begin to join in. Tito seems to pick up the beat most quickly and is able to carry on even after Ms. Mendez stops unexpectedly. She asks, "Tito, can you make a pattern that follows the same rule but has us do different things?"

Tito thinks for a bit, then touches his head once and touches his toes three times. "Great work, Tito! You touched your head once, just like we snapped once. Then you touched your toes three times, just like we clapped three times."

Ms. Mendez can see that talking about and exploring patterns is deepening the children's understanding of them when she observes Alicia in the science center a few weeks later. Alicia is thumbing through a stack of cards with pictures of fruits and vegetables and creating a line of them on the floor. Ms. Mendez watches as she carefully chooses which card to add next to her lineup, even referencing a nonfiction book about produce next to her. When Alicia pauses, Ms. Mendez inquires what she's working on. "I'm making a pattern that goes *fruit, vegetable, fruit, vegetable*." Pointing to each card in her line, she continues, "See? Orange, carrot, apple, potato, pear, beans." Ms. Mendez exclaims, "That is such a great tricky pattern! People are really going to have to think hard to see it. I wonder if the other children will be able to name some different fruits and vegetables to extend your pattern even further."

Children move from being Pattern Detectives (recognizing patterns) to Pattern Makers (creating patterns). This evolution follows a predictable trajectory.

Recognizing patterns means being aware of and identifying regularity and sequence. As Ms. Mendez realized, children need many experiences identifying and talking about pattern rules before they can understand them. Engage children in conversations that invite them to think about familiar basic repeating sequences, like those in their own daily routines (for example, wake up, eat breakfast with Dad, go to school) or predictable lines in a storybook.

Small blue triangle, large red square, small blue triangle, large red square, small blue triangle, large red square

Copying patterns, or duplicating them, follows fairly quickly after recognizing them; in fact, many children may intuitively join in on the refrain of a favorite song or recurring movements of a finger play before they can name the elements of the pattern. Build on their understanding through authentic, play-based experiences and conversations that emphasize pattern structure, such as stringing beads on a necklace. Begin with simple *ab* patterns—in which two elements alternate—that focus on a single attribute, like color: "Isla, the rule for your necklace seems to be *green, yellow, green, yellow, green, yellow.*" As children's understanding grows, you can introduce more complex patterns, such as *abc* (*red, blue, yellow, red, blue, yellow*) or *abb* (*red, blue, blue, red, blue, blue*), or patterns that involve two or even three attributes, like the figure on page 32 that involves size, color, *and* shape.

Extending patterns calls for showing or predicting what comes next or naming a missing element in a pattern. In the vignette on pages 31–32, Ginny has reached this stage: she realizes that she and Tito can join the end of the line to continue the pattern Ms. Mendez created based on what shirts the children were wearing. However, she will likely need many more concrete experiences playing with patterns before she understands that she could also replace Orin, Eli, or Chandler (who are all wearing striped shirts) and still keep the *striped shirt, solid shirt* pattern, or that she and Tito could have gone to the front of the line and extended the pattern that way. These more complex extensions depend on children developing and deepening their understanding of the rules that govern patterns, including these:

■ Pattern units must be repeated at least three times before there is enough evidence to understand a pattern's structure and pre es next. For example, some children in Ms. Mendez's class may initially have thought that the pattern was *boy, girl* because

the first two sets of children did fit that pattern. The third set, however, clearly broke that potential pattern but cemented the pattern of *striped shirt, solid shirt* that Ms. Mendez had in mind.

■ Pattern units can be generalized. That is, we can classify repeating pattern units with letters (such as *ab, abba,* or *abc*). So, for example, *red, blue* is an *ab* pattern, but so is *blue triangle, red square* or *striped shirt, solid shirt*. The two elements in each of those units could also be flipped, and each would still be an *ab* pattern. Being able to make this kind of generalization is a sign that a child's abstract reasoning is developing.

Translating patterns, or using new materials or ways to represent a pattern, indicates further development of abstract thinking and the understanding that there are many different ways to symbolize a generalized pattern unit. When Ms. Mendez challenged Tito to re-create her pattern using different actions, they both followed the *abbb* rule using different elements: her *a* element was a snap while his was touching his head, and her *b* element was clapping while his was touching his toes.

Creating patterns calls for higher-level thinking, as Alicia's *fruit, vegetable* pattern shows. To make her own original pattern, she has taken her understanding of how the rule for an *ab* pattern works and used it in a unique and complex way that shows her knowledge of the differences between fruits and vegetables.

Recognizing, copying, extending, translating, and creating patterns involve cognitive understanding that is not tied to any particular language. In other words, children may well be able to understand and use patterns even if they cannot express this knowledge with words in English. Be alert to nonverbal and performance cues that demonstrate children's understanding.

Exploring Growing Patterns

The snapshot of Ms. Mendez's classroom deals entirely with repeating patterns, but young children also need experiences with growing patterns. *Growing patterns* are sequences where the pattern is added to (increased) or taken away from (decreased) by a consistent, predictable size or amount. This kind of pattern can be found all around us, and the most basic growing pattern is our counting system. Each number grows by one more than the number before it:

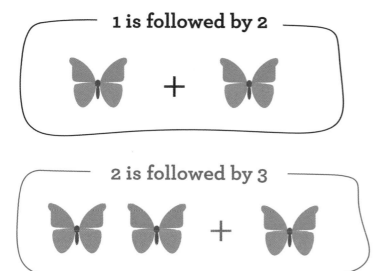

When children understand that counting by ones follows the rule of adding a quantity of one to the previous number, they eventually see that this rule applies for both small numbers they are used to dealing with ("Seven comes after six, because six plus one is seven!") and larger two- and three-digit numbers they will learn about later. Comprehension of this concept also lays the groundwork for the math learning with growing number patterns children do when they are older, like adding quantities larger than one when counting by twos, fives, or even tens. Developmentally, most children are in kindergarten or the early primary grades before they can recognize and become fluent with growing number patterns.

Many songs and stories also use growing patterns, and they are a great way to help children understand this concept. Some, like the cumulative rhyme "There Was an Old Lady Who Swallowed a Fly," can even jump-start young children's thinking about how repeating and growing patterns work together. While the song doesn't explicitly talk about numbers, with each stanza, the number of creatures in the Old Lady's belly increases by one. The number of lines in the refrain increases as well: it repeats each creature she swallows and then adds the new creature.

PATTERN DETECTIVES

Inspired by *Pete the Cat: I Love My White Shoes* / Eric Litwin, illus. James Dean

The Story

Pete the Cat loves his white shoes. As Pete goes walking down the street, he steps in all kinds of things that make his shoes change colors. Instead of getting upset, Pete sings about how much he loves his shoes whether they are white, red, brown, or blue!

Consider the Math Concept

The enduring strength and enjoyment of books like this is that they are strongly patterned in almost every respect. While true with any reading experience, it is especially important to revisit a book several times with children when asking them to notice things like patterns. There is a lot to take in, and children learn through repetition. Being able to name patterns and the rules that govern them is a skill that develops over time as a result of many conversations. It is up to you to encourage, facilitate, and reinforce conversations that invite children to explore the many different forms patterns can take.

This book features several kinds of strong, predictable repeating patterns in

- Story structure: The plot follows a repeating pattern—Pete has shoes that are one color; he steps in something that makes them change color; he sings about how he love his new color of shoes; and this cycle starts over again.

- Sounds: The text makes extensive use of repetitive sound patterns including *rhyme* (repeats the same end sound), *alliteration* (repeats the same initial sound), and *rhythm and beat* (repeats the flow of words and sentences as they are read aloud).

- Sentence structure and meaning: Each time a change is forced on Pete, the same upbeat message repeats with a question ("Did Pete cry?") followed by an exclamation ("Goodness, no!").

- Text and illustration design: The way the words and sentences are arranged on each page follows a consistent pattern. Key details of the illustrations also repeat; for example, Pete's shoes are identical in appearance on each page except for their color.

Materials

- Large easel, dry erase board, or chart paper
- Markers

This activity can work in small and whole group settings.

Explore and Investigate Together

After looking and listening, children will soon join in, feeling excited and confident that they know what comes next. When children join in on the refrain in the story, ask them how they knew what to say. Before the next iteration of the pattern begins, ask children if they can guess what is going to happen next. Talk about how finding patterns and using them to make good predictions is an important part of making sense of stories and math.

Ask the children to think about the story and to point out any patterns they noticed. Keep your questions and comments as open ended as possible ("What did you see happening again and again? What did you hear happening again and again?"), but target a specific example if children are struggling to begin ("Pete is standing on this big pile of blueberries. What do you think is going to happen next?"). Ask how they can know the right answer even before turning the page.

When the children identify a pattern, record their answers on the chart paper. Take time to invite feedback by asking other children about their thoughts: "Amal noticed that Pete keeps stepping in things as he walks. That's a really important pattern in the story. He steps in strawberries or mud while walking along. What happens each time he steps in something?"

Talk About the Math

Children who are just beginning to recognize and name patterns will need specific prompts. Reinforce their responses by echoing and paraphrasing them.

- Nadia, you said that every time you hear "Goodness, no!," you get ready to sing Pete's song. You are a real pattern detective! You noticed that two things get repeated together—that phrase and the song.

Encourage children who can recognize and name patterns to extend them.

- What if Pete's shoes turned green? What might he have stepped in?
- What do you think might happen if Pete stepped in a puddle of purple paint? What would he say?
- What else could Pete step in? What color would his shoes turn?

Individualize the Activity

- Children are sensitive to noticing when an established sequence of actions or events changes. Once children have heard you read the story many times and are able to join in, deliberately make a mistake (such as by saying "goodness, yes" or singing the song with the wrong color of shoes) while reading the text and wait for the children to correct you. This strategy gets the children thinking of what they know about the way a pattern works.

- Invite children who are confident at naming and recognizing the pattern of the story to extend it. Provide them with paper, markers, and pencils and ask them to write and/or draw their ideas for what else Pete could step in, what color his shoes would be, and what song he would sing.

- Read other books in the *Pete the Cat* series and explore with the children how they are the same as and different from *Pete the Cat: I Love My White Shoes*. For example, both this book and *Pete the Cat and His Four Groovy Buttons* follow an *abc* pattern:

  (a) Pete sings about how much he likes his shoes and the color they are (his buttons and how many there are).

  (b) The color of the shoes (number of buttons) changes.

  (c) Pete sings about how he likes the new color (number).

More Books

Brown Bear, Brown Bear, What Do You See? / Bill Martin, Jr., illus. Eric Carle

The Pout-Pout Fish / Deborah Diesen, illus. Dan Hanna

Six Dots: A Story of Young Louis Braille / Jen Bryant, illus. Boris Kulikov

STAIRSTEP STORY PATTERNS

Inspired by *The Napping House* / Audrey Wood, illus. Don Wood

The Story

On a rainy afternoon, a granny, a boy, and other creatures who live in the house are peacefully sleeping in a pile on a cozy bed. But when a wakeful flea joins them, they won't be napping for long . . .

Consider the Math Concept

This is an excellent example of how a rich children's book doesn't need to explicitly have numbers in it to be mathematized. The story itself is cumulative and illustrates a growing (plus-one) pattern: each time a new character shows up, the text repeats the same sentence pattern to introduce (add) a new creature to those who are already sleeping on the bed. As the list of sleepers grows, so do the lines of text on the page and the number of characters in the illustrations.

Note: *Growing pattern* describes situations that count up (add) and count down (subtract). Typically, children are close to age 6 before they can readily understand or express the plus-one rule, much less extend or create a growing pattern. However, talking about and acting out these patterns is engaging for children and builds their understanding.

PLAN

Materials

For each set of manipulatives, you'll need

- Printouts of pictures (about 2" × 2") to represent each of the characters in the story:
  - 6 of the granny
  - 5 of the boy
  - 4 of the dog
  - 3 of the cat
  - 2 of the mouse
  - 1 of the flea
- 21 blocks
- Tape

This activity works best going from whole group to small group settings. Start out by working with all the children, but move to work with small groups as the children make and discuss their own models of the growing pattern using manipulatives. Look online to find printable pictures that can be cut into cards to represent the characters from the book or draw your own. Tape these pictures onto the blocks so the children can stack them. Be sure to create enough sets for children to work with in small groups.

Explore and Investigate Together

To help children focus on the patterns in the book, ask them what kinds of things they notice repeating in the story and the illustrations. What changes each time a new character comes in?

After discussing their observations about the story, bring out the character blocks you have prepared. Invite the children to help you use them to figure out what special kind of pattern is in the story. Revisit the story with the children, pausing after each character climbs onto the bed to sleep. Begin with the page that shows the granny on the bed and ask one of the children to choose the right character block and to set it out to show that granny is the only one sleeping. Turn to the next page and ask, "Who is napping now? How can we line up our characters in the next column to show what is happening to the number of sleepers?" You may want to model the first few columns, but engage the children in guiding your actions rather than immediately showing them where to place the blocks. Continue going through each of the illustrations and have the children use the character blocks to build a simple pictograph, column by column.

Talk About the Math

To help children make discoveries and construct their own understanding of the growing pattern in the story, use open-ended questions and prompts like the following:

- A third character has just entered the room. We need to make a new column. Who goes first, on the bottom? Who comes next? And how about on top?
- What do you notice when looking at the character pictures across the same row? Tell me why you think that is.
- What do you notice about how our pictograph is changing?
- Danai, you just said that the pictograph sort of looks like a staircase. Does anyone have any ideas about why it looks that way?

Individualize the Activity

- If children find stacking the blocks frustrating, have them work with just the character card printouts and create columns with them on a flat surface. You might also provide a six by six grid to help children keep the cards aligned.
- To make the growing pattern concept more concrete for children, have them act out the story before introducing the pictograph activity. Keep the emphasis on the pattern by narrating the story and having children pantomime. Give six children the roles of the characters to act out the story and explain to the rest of the children that they have an important job as the audience to answer your questions each round: "How many creatures are sleeping now? How many more is that than there were before?"
- Some children might be ready or express interest in making their own growing pattern story. Encourage them to create one by writing, drawing, acting it out, or using manipulatives. If they would like to, they can share their growing pattern story with the rest of the class.

More Books

Down by the Barn / Will Hillenbrand

The Mitten / Jan Brett

The Water Hole / Graeme Base

CYCLES AS PATTERNS

Inspired by *The Growing Story* / Ruth Krauss, illus. Helen Oxenbury

The Story

A little boy lives on a farm where everything around him is growing, making him wonder "Am I growing too?" His mother keeps reassuring him that he is growing, but the boy can't see how he is changing the way he can see changes happening in his puppy, the barnyard chicks, and all the plants and trees.

Consider the Math Concept

This story offers rich connections to the way the mathematical question "what comes next?" can be found in the growth and changes we see in plants and animals, including humans! It also explores how plants, animals, and humans grow and change differently. For example, while the tree, the puppy, and the boy all increase in size during the story, their rate of growth varies enormously. Physical growth in the puppy and seasonal changes in the tree progress much faster than growth and change do in the little boy.

Focusing on growing patterns is typically most appropriate for children who are in kindergarten and the early primary grades. Their ability to understand growth over time is developing rapidly as is their understanding of cause and effect. By kindergarten, many children can use the clearly marked stages of the life cycles of plants and living creatures to generalize the way an individual living thing grows to maturity in a predictable sequence. Talking about cycles is a natural way to develop children's understanding of ordinal words, including *first, second, third, next, after,* and *finally.*

Where's the Math?

Materials

- Heavy cardstock or cardboard, such as from a tissue box or milk carton
- Scissors
- Tape
- Paper cut into 4"× 4" squares or similar
- Markers and crayons
- Glue

This activity works best going from whole group to small group settings. Start out by working with all the children to open the discussion and model the cycle box (described on page 46), but work with small groups as the children make and discuss their own cycle boxes.

On the paper squares, draw an arrow pointing to the left with the label *before* and another arrow pointing right with the label *after*. There should be plenty of space in the box for children to write a few words and draw a picture. Ahead of the activity, prepare four of these paper squares with pictures that show the life cycle stages of one of the creatures from the story. For example, if you choose to model the cycle box for a chicken, the four stages might be a drawing of an egg, one of a baby chick, one of a young chicken, and one of an adult chicken that can lay eggs. Hold off labeling the stages with words; you'll do that together with the children.

Explore and Investigate Together

Once the children are familiar with the story, ask them for their thoughts about why the book is called *The Growing Story*. They may first talk about how the boy grows, but be sure they also think about how the chicks, puppy, and pear tree also grow and change. Discuss how all living things follow the same pattern: they begin very small and then grow bigger until they reach adult size. The adult plant or animal can then produce eggs or seeds that will grow into a new

generation. Explain that a pattern that goes around again and again, like these growing events or the four seasons, is called a *cycle*. Use the illustrations to show one cycle, such as the tree in different seasons or the puppy growing into a dog.

Begin by modeling how to create a cycle box with the whole group, doing the actual work of putting together the cycle box so the children can watch but calling on them to give you help with the directions. Cut heavy cardstock into a long, thick strip, then fold the strip into four equal panels. Lay the strip flat again after creasing it and set it aside. Bring out the paper squares depicting the four stages of the life cycle of an animal from the book that you prepared ahead of the activity. Display the squares in a random order in a way that is visible to all of the children. Explain to the children what the before and after arrows on each square mean, then ask them to help you decide what to name each stage and in what order the life stages happen. Once the order of the life stages has been determined, have the children help you glue them on the cardstock strip you folded earlier, one in each of the four panels. Refold the cardstock strip and tape the ends of the first and last panels together to create a box that can stand.

Invite a few of the children to turn the box in their hands and to name each of the stages in the chicken's life cycle. As they do, emphasize the before and after sequence of the stages and how the rule for cycles is that the stages must occur in a predictable fixed order; a chick can only hatch after an adult chicken has laid an egg.

Work in small groups to have the children make their own cycle boxes for another creature or plant from the book. You might create a reference chart that shows terms for each stage. A flower, for example, could have *seed*, *sprout* (or *shoot*), *bud* (or *blossom*), and *flower*. Provide children with nonfiction books with realistic photographs and sketches of the plant or animal they are creating a cycle box for to reference as they draw their own pictures. Encourage them to look closely at these books to observe details they can use to help them draw as accurately as possible.

Talk About the Math

While children may be able to recite the different stages of growth for a specific plant or animal, the concept that each stage involves changes is abstract. Ask questions and start conversations to facilitate deeper thinking about the growth cycle, like the following:

- What does it mean to be a baby or a grown-up (adult)?
- What are some things you can do now that you couldn't do when you were a baby? What are some things you want to be able to do when you are bigger that you can't do now?
- Can you think of something you do each day that needs to happen in a specific order?

Individualize the Activity

- If identifying and ordering stages of growth into the correct pattern using a cycle box is challenging for some children, focus on how much they have developed themselves since they were born. Use sentence frames like these for children to complete: "When I was little, I couldn't _____. Now that I am older, I can _____." You might ask families to bring in photos of the children.

- If there are children in your class who speak a home language other than English, before introducing this activity, research the words in their home languages for the various plants, living creatures, and growth stages you will be exploring and using as labels. Families are a great resource to provide the vocabulary for children's home languages.

- Give children who excel at identifying and ordering the life cycle stages of plants and animals explored in the story the opportunity to choose a plant or animal they're interested in and create a cycle box with drawings and labels they come up with. An activity like this could be connected to a study about animal families or an inquiry about butterflies or another specific creature. Provide resources for children to research how long each stage lasts for different animals or plants. For example, robins grow from a hatched egg to an adult in about three weeks. Most dogs mature within a year, but each breed differs.

More Books

Goodbye Summer, Hello Autumn / Kenard Pak

Plant the Tiny Seed / Christie Matheson

Pumpkin Pumpkin / Jeanne Titherington

AND . . . ACTION!

Inspired by "Bingo"

The Game

Action songs that use sequence and repetition, like the well-known song about a farmer and his dog, "Bingo," allow children to use their bodies to explore and expand their understanding of pattern structures. They're also a wonderful way to support children's physical development and thinking skills—not to mention an effective way to encourage self-regulation.

Consider the Math Concept

Classic sing-along games like "Five Little Monkeys," "Five Little Ducks," and "Un Elefante Se Balanceaba" wear their connection to math front and center (counting up and down), but you might be surprised that "Bingo," which doesn't explicitly use numbers, has math embedded in it. "Bingo" is a highly effective way to help children understand and create patterns. The song has four lines that make up a stanza where children spell out the dog's name. Each time the stanza is repeated, one more letter is clapped instead of spoken. "Bingo" is both a repeating pattern *and* a growing pattern—one that children can literally hear and feel as two claps become three when they go from *clap, clap, N-G-O* to *clap, clap, clap, G-O*. Keep in mind that much of the built-in learning power of these songs comes from you and the children doing them together, not just listening to or watching them be performed by others.

· PLAN ·

Materials

- Large easel, dry erase board, or chart paper
- Markers

This activity can work in small and whole group settings. Write out the base stanza of the song, labeling each line as an element in an *abcb* pattern:

> *a:* There was a farmer, who had a dog,
>
> *b:* And Bingo was his name, oh!
>
> *c:* B-I-N-G-O, B-I-N-G-O, B-I-N-G-O,
>
> *b:* And Bingo was his name, oh!

On another piece of chart paper or at the other end of the dry erase board, draw a table with three columns labeled *Repeated Words, Repeated Actions,* and *Changes in Each Stanza.*

Explore and Investigate Together

While young children might intuitively recognize that this and other action songs follow a pattern, they need multiple conversations about how the words and actions are structured to understand how repetition and sequence make it easy to predict what they need to do next as the song continues. Ask the children to think about the different elements of the song. What things do they notice repeating? What things change? As they give answers, write them in the table, asking the children to confirm what category each element falls under. Use their responses and the table to get the children thinking about the repetitions and sequence. With younger children, the conversation will likely focus more on the repeated words and actions. If the children are comfortable extending and translating patterns, focus on the *abcb* pattern unit that the song follows.

Talk About the Math

The more children are motivated to express their thinking, the more they learn, so keep this a playful and engaging activity rather than a lesson. As children make their observations and feel the excitement of making a discovery, build on what they say to make their points more precise.

- Rovena, you said the name *Bingo* is used five times in the song. Did anybody notice some different ways in *how* the name is used?

- A few of you noticed that the line "And Bingo was his name, oh!" stays exactly the same each time in every stanza. What do you notice happening to the line where Bingo's name is spelled out in each stanza?

- Can anybody think of a way to change the clap pattern to another sound pattern? How about a movement pattern?

- Sometimes we sing this song using our own names. What parts of this song pattern do we keep? What do we change? Is it easier to use long names or short names? Why do you think that is?

Individualize the Activity

- If some children struggle with the *abcb* pattern unit of "Bingo," work up to this activity by giving them plenty of opportunity to explore books, poems, and songs that follow a simpler pattern (like *ab*). Use the chart to get the children thinking about the repetitions and sequence that they should be looking for. Only discuss the pattern unit with children who are already comfortable with extending and translating patterns. With younger children, focus on the repeated words and clapping actions. You might have a small group of children demonstrate one or two rounds of the song to jumpstart their thinking.

- Invite children's families to come in and share action songs in their home languages and from their cultures. Analyze them for repeating patterns, growing patterns, or both!

- Challenge children by doing a silly version of a familiar action song, like "Head, Shoulders, Knees, and Toes." A silly version might mix up the established pattern of going from head to toes. Take the time to talk about why the silly version is so tricky, including how the well-known sequence of the lyrics is broken and how the logic of moving from head down to toes is lost.

Related Books

Baby Shark / John John Bajet

Head, Shoulders, Knees and Toes . . . / illus. Annie Kubler

I'm a Little Teapot! / illus. Annie Kubler

Chapter Three

NUMBER SENSE

HOW MANY DO WE HAVE, NEED, OR WANT?

Math Concepts Explored in this Chapter

- Abstraction
- Cardinality
- Counting
- Number operation
- Number sense

- Number words
- Numbers
- Object order irrelevance
- One-to-one correspondence
- Quantity

- Rational counting
- Rote counting
- Stable order
- Subitize

Every day, you encounter situations where you need or want to know *how many:* Do I have enough pencils so that each of my 20 students gets one? Should I put one or two spoonfuls of sugar in my tea? How many families still need to turn in signed permission slips for the field trip? Children are instinctively curious about the quantities of things in their day-to-day lives as well as the quantities they notice in pictures, songs, and stories. They naturally compare and label when they think someone has *more* than they do or when they say *no more* when they are finished eating.

Exploring Counting

The children in Mrs. Pryor's class, who are all 5 years old or will be soon, are listening intently as she reads them *Feast for 10*, a book about a family as they grocery shop, prepare a meal, and eat it together. This is their third read-aloud of this story, and before starting, Mrs. Pryor invites the children to ask questions and make comments when she pauses at the end of each page.

"One cart into the grocery store," Mrs. Pryor reads. Kiera thinks that counting the people on the page is much more interesting. She jumps up and points as she counts, "One, two, three, four, five, six!" Following Kiera's lead, Mrs. Pryor says, "That's right, Kiera! There are six people at the grocery store. I wonder what else we see here that we can count." On another page, Shane points at the pickles going in the shopping cart and says, "They are getting lots. That's good, 'cause I like pickles." Mrs. Pryor responds to Shane's interest, asking, "Do you think seven pickles will be enough for everyone?"

On the last page where all of the characters are sitting down, Franklin wonders why there are only nine chairs if there are 10 people. "Oh, I see! The baby is sitting on her mommy's lap because she's just little," he says, gesturing with his hands. "But I'm big. I'm four!" Meanwhile, Colette is counting the pieces of chicken on the big platter the dad is holding. "One, two, three, four, five—oops, wait," she says, tapping her finger on each piece of chicken as she counts again. "It's four!"

When they reach the end of the book, Shane says, "I love that story! It's just like going to the store!" Mrs. Pryor smiles to herself. The actual text in the book is very spare; each page has a numeral, a number word, and a set of things being counted. The real story, she thinks, is the one that the children told each other as they made connections between the detailed illustrations and their everyday lives.

Like Mrs. Pryor, it's important to understand that there are two types of counting:

- **Rote counting** is memorizing and reciting number words in the right order.
- **Rational counting** is accurately attaching a number word to items in a collection to indicate how many of something there is.

While rote counting is an important foundation of rational counting, rational counting skills are what children need to make meaningful sense of quantity—or how many. To bridge rote counting with rational counting and to support children's *number sense*—that is, their ability to understand how many items are in a set and how to use number words to convey that quantity—it is essential to emphasize that *something* needs to be counted. When talking about math with children, numbers need to be defined as another kind of attribute. *Three,* like *colorful* or *wooden,* is an adjective that describes an object or set of objects. Unless it is describing something, there is no such thing as *three.*

Numbers make it possible to compare quantities and see relationships between them. The best way to build that understanding in children is to do as Mrs. Pryor did—by having conversations that connect numbers and quantities with real-life experiences. Young children are just beginning to connect the words they say (number words) to the concept those words represent (quantity). The process begins early—brain research shows that humans are born with the ability to *subitize,* or to see a small number of objects and be able to tell how many there are without counting them (Antell & Keating 1983). However, connecting the number words with those small quantities doesn't happen until children are about 2 years old (Clements & Sarama 2010). Because numbers are an abstract attribute (whereas color and shape are concrete attributes that can readily be seen), children need many, many experiences before this connection between the words and the concept becomes clear. To help children grasp the concept that quantity is the focus, numerals and number words should be shown with dots or some other tangible representation—that *something*—children can physically count.

Counting with Dual Language Learners

Dual language learners have an additional challenge when learning how to count because number words change from language to language. If you have ever tried shopping in a foreign country, you know how difficult it is to convey how many of an object you want or to ask how much something costs without knowing the right word to use. In fact, it is likely you resort to pointing and using your fingers. It's important to pay attention to gestures and other strategies children who are dual language learners or nonverbal use to indicate quantity, even if they don't yet know the number word. It's also important to help them map their home language terms to the English number words. Engage with families, work with a volunteer translator, and research online to learn how to say and write numbers in the home languages of the children you teach.

Developing Rational Counting Skills

As young children progress from rote counting to rational counting, they gradually develop an understanding of these five principles.

Stable order: Number words must be said in the same sequence every time because they have a fixed meaning as a growing pattern. Each number in the sequence is one more than the number before it—2 is one more than 1, just as 215 is predictably one more than 214.

One-to-one correspondence: Only one number word is named for each object being counted. To help children avoid counting the same object more than once, encourage them to point at each object as they use a number word to count it.

Object order irrelevance: No matter how objects in a group are arranged or in what order they are counted, the quantity of objects will not change. You can show children this principle by having them count a group of objects to determine the quantity. Then ask them to mix up that same group of objects and count them again. What did they find? To keep track of which items they have counted and which they have not, encourage the children to push each item to one side of the table as they count it.

Cardinality: The last number word said when counting represents the total quantity of objects counted. When counting, a child will say a number word for each of the objects being counted. Once she has counted the last object, that number not only names the order of that specific object, it also tells the child how many objects there are in the set: "I have one . . . two . . . three teacups. There are three teacups!"

Abstraction: Any set of objects that can be seen, touched, heard, or even imagined can be counted, whether it is made up of objects that are similar to or completely different from one another.

It is critical to intentionally build on children's number sense by encouraging and exploring the many questions young children have about *how many* as they read, play, and go about their daily routines. As you help children link numbers to the objects they see, the ideas they have, and the questions they ask, you are handing them powerful tools that they will use to meaningfully understand quantities for the rest of their lives.

SOME FROGS HERE, SOME FROGS THERE

Inspired by *Five Green and Speckled Frogs: A Count-and-Sing Book* / Priscilla Burris

The Story

This book is a new spin on a classic children's song. Five frogs sit together on a log, eating bugs. One by one, they jump off the log into the pool.

Consider the Math Concept

This sing-along book makes it very clear that counting isn't just reciting number words. The rules that govern counting are illustrated through both repeating patterns (one frog jumps into the pond at a time) and growing patterns (the number of frogs left on the log) in each stanza. Notice that the frogs are not labeled with numbers. As you prepare for the activity, keep this in mind. This is an important opportunity to show children firsthand the order irrelevance principle—it doesn't matter which frog jumps in first or last. Each time a frog jumps, there is one less frog on the log and one more in the water.

PLAN

Materials

- Large easel, dry erase board, or chart paper
- Markers
- Index cards
- Masking tape
- Frog puppets (optional)

This activity is for whole group settings. The children can either act out the story themselves or use frog puppets (stuffed animals, felt cutouts, stick figures). Use masking tape to mark off a "log" and a "cool pool" on the floor. On a large easel, draw a chart with three columns labeled *Frogs on the Log, Frogs in the Pool,* and *Total Frogs*. Create two sets of cards, each with a numeral 1 through 5. Include dots (or even frog stickers!) on each card to show the quantity.

Explore and Investigate Together

As you read the story, draw children's attention to the fact that each time a frog leaves the log to go into the pool, the number of frogs on the log changes. Point out that while the number of frogs on the log is going down, the number of frogs in the pond is going up. Ask the children what they think that means for the total number of frogs—those on the log *and* those on the pond, together. Do they think the total number changes or stays the same even when the frogs are in different places? As you explore these details of the story, children begin to see how counting is related to adding and subtracting.

Divide the children into two groups, one group of five children to play the frogs (or to have responsibility for the frog puppets) and the remaining children to be the audience. Explain that each group has different but equally important roles: the children playing the frogs will act out what is happening in the song for everyone to see, while the children in the audience will count the number of frogs on the log and in the pool, total them, and help you fill in the chart. Pass out one number card to each child in the audience. Using number cards allows children to focus on the math rather than the effort it might take to write the numeral.

Direct all of the children playing or manipulating the frogs to start together in a row on the log. Before beginning the song, guide the children in the audience to count the number of frogs sitting on the log together, and invite anyone who thinks they are holding the right number card to stand up. Because there are two sets of cards distributed, two children will stand up each time you prompt this question for each number. Have one of them place their number card on the chart in the first column labeled *Frogs on the Log* (helping them secure it in place with tape), and reassure the second child that they will have a chance to use their card and to keep their eyes and ears open. At this time, summarize and build on what the children have discovered: "So we have five frogs on the log. Right now, there are no frogs in the pool. So, our total number of frogs is five." Write the numeral 5 in the third column labeled *Frogs Total.*

As you and the children sing the first stanza of the song together, point to one child on the log as her cue to move over to the pool. At the end of each stanza, bring the children's attention back to the chart. Ask the children in the audience to count the number of frogs on the log and to stand if they think they are holding the right number card, then invite one child to place that card on the chart in the first column. Ask the children to do the same for the second column (Frogs in the Pool). For the third column (Frogs Total), guide the children in the audience to count both the number of frogs on the log and the number of frogs in the pool. When they conclude the total is five, write in the numeral. Repeat this process for each stanza of the song. As the stanzas progress, be sure to randomly point to children who make up the line of frogs on the log to reinforce the order irrelevance principle; don't just go down the line.

Talk About the Math

Offer specific feedback on the children's responses, and help them focus on rational counting.

- **Mr. Hariri:** Our second frog has jumped off the log and into the pool. How many frogs are on the log now? (*Leads the children in counting them.*) Three, that's right, everyone! Who has a number card for three?
  Bharucha: I do! (*Holds up his number card, which has the numeral 2 on it.*)
  Mr. Hariri: Let's look carefully at your card. Count how many dots there are.
  Bharucha: (*Uses his finger to point to each dot as he counts.*) One, two. Two!
  Mr. Hariri: Right! And how many frogs did we count on the log?
  Bharucha: Three . . . oh, I don't have the right card. (*Sits back down.*)
- We have two frogs left on the log and three swimming in the pool. What do you think is going to happen next? What numbers do you think we'll need to record on our chart?
- That was some excellent counting, everyone! Now, let's take a look at the numbers we recorded on our chart. What do you notice?

Individualize the Activity

- Young preschoolers are still developing solid number sense for four and five, so keep to activities that call for counting no more than five objects. If children are struggling with the activity, begin with a smaller quantity and work up to a larger quantity. As children's number sense for five is consolidated, do similar activities with the many counting books and songs that go to 10.
- At first, some children may not be clear on whether you're asking them to count the number of frogs on the log or those in the pool. Use visual supports, like pictures and gestures, to support their understanding.
- Challenge children to make up their own version of a song or story that counts up rather than down.

More Books

One Duck Stuck: A Mucky Ducky Counting Book / Phyllis Root, illus. Jane Chapman

Over in a River: Flowing Out to the Sea / Marianne Berkes, illus. Jill Dubin

Un Elefante: Numbers/Números / Patty Rodriguez and Ariana Stein, illus. Citlali Reyes

A TREAT TO EAT

Inspired by *Baby Goes to Market* / Atinuke, illus. Angela Brooksbank

The Story

Baby and Mama go shopping for food at the bustling marketplace. As they visit the different stalls, many things end up in Mama's basket—some of which she didn't put there!

Consider the Math Concept

This vibrant book celebrates southwestern Nigerian food and culture while exploring counting principles. The story describes fruits, vegetables, sweets, and other wares of different shapes and colors, specifically showing how Baby eats one of each item of food and then sneaks the remaining number (which decreases by one each time) into Mama's basket without her knowing. The minus-one pattern we see unfold illustrates an important relationship in our counting system: each number is *one more* than the one before it, which means each number is also *one less* than the number after it. Reflecting on number relationships this way helps children make meaning of counting and our number system. As they see Baby receive a certain amount of food, eat a certain amount of food, and put the remainder in the basket, children are also exploring the fundamentals of adding and subtracting.

PLAN

Materials

- Shopping list with no more than six familiar items on it and with drawings or photos of each item next to the word
- Local grocery store ads
- Large and small bowls
- Serving spoons

This activity works best going from whole group to small group settings. Make or collect enough copies of the shopping list and grocery store ads for children to share in groups of no more than two or three.

Explore and Investigate Together

Explain to the children that many adults use lists and grocery store ads to plan what they will buy when they go shopping. Go over the different items on the shopping list you've shared with them, pointing out different details and explanations: "I'm going to make noodle soup with vegetables for dinner this week. There are four people in my family, and to make enough soup for everyone, I need two boxes of noodles, four carrots, one onion, and two boxes of vegetable broth." Point out how preparing a meal always involves figuring out how many of something you need.

Tell the children that as a group, you are going to make a list of foods to buy at the local grocery store so that you can make a fruit salad or a healthy snack mix for everyone to eat. As a class, first decide which you'd like to make. Divide the children into four to five small groups to look over the ads and have each group choose an item that will be part of the shopping list and their snack. (Be sure the ads feature food you can actually buy for this activity.)

After purchasing the items on the grocery list, prepare and cut up each food item as needed and place each type of food into its own large bowl with a serving spoon. Ask children to describe what's in the big bowls. They will notice that there are many pieces of fruit or cereal and will likely wonder "How many are there?" and "How many can I have?"

Provide each child with a small bowl and let her decide what her specific fruit salad or snack mix will include. Prompt the children to think about and explain how many of each food item they want to include in their snack.

Talk About the Math

As children choose what foods to include in their snack and count aloud, ask questions and make comments to help them consider the mathematical aspects of their recipe more closely.

- William, how many different kinds of fruit did you put in your salad?

- I heard you counting the different fruits you have in your recipe, Noah. There are three strawberry slices, four blueberries, and two chunks of mango. I wonder how many pieces of fruit are in your salad in total? How many will there be after you eat a piece?

- Talia and Elinor, you both have raisins in your snack mix. How many raisins do you each have? Who has more raisins? How do you know? How many raisins do you have if you put them all together?

Learning about quantity and counting requires a lot of experience seeing, touching, and talking about objects and events in daily life. Encourage children to think about and find the math in their own day-to-day routines and experiences at home and school.

- I wonder how many different ways we can eat the same fruit. We have apples in our fruits salads and we also have applesauce at snack time. That's two ways we eat apples. Can anyone think of more?

- How many people are in your family? If you were making a shopping list for your family, how many bananas would you need to buy so everyone could have one?

Individualize the Activity

- For new counters, you might place number cards with dots by each bowl of ingredients to specify how many pieces of each fruit children should count out and put in their salad.

- Prefill small bowls with certain amounts of each fruit. Before they eat it, ask the children to count how many pieces of each fruit is in their bowl.

- Challenge children to compare "recipes" and talk about who has more and who has less of a certain food. Consider asking some basic joining and separating problems that call for addition and subtraction, like "If you have five strawberry slices and you gave me two, how many slices of strawberry would you have left? How do you know?"

More Books

Grandma's Tiny House: A Counting Story! / JaNay Brown-Wood, illus. Priscilla Burris

How Many Jelly Beans? / Andrea Menotti, illus. Yancey Labat

Soup Day / Melissa Iwai

COUNTING BY FEET

Inspired by *One Is a Snail, Ten Is a Crab: A Counting by Feet Book* / April Pulley Sayre and Jeff Sayre, illus. Randy Cecil

The Story

Four is a dog and eight is a spider—but why? Find out the importance of knowing what exactly is being counted with the delightfully zany text and illustrations in this counting book set at the beach.

Consider the Math Concept

When counting, it's important not only to name the number word but also to identify *what* is being counted. *One Is a Snail* proves this point on each page as a number is assigned to an animal without the text explaining *why*. Only the arrows pointing to each animal's feet make it clear that's what is being counted! Knowing this, it makes perfect sense why one is a snail: a snail has one foot. The text gets more playful, combining creatures to make odd-numbered feet, like getting to nine by counting a snail's one foot *and* a spider's eight feet.

This book is also a wonderful introduction to the growing pattern structure of our base-10 number system, meaning that all numbers are represented using 10 numerals, 0 through 9.

While exploring how counting follows the plus-one rule, for example, older children who read this book begin to see how the rule that gives us 2, 3, 4, and so on also applies to numbers in the tens place: 20 is 2 tens; 30 is 3 tens; and 40 is 4 tens. This is akin to kindergartners learning that 10 ones is the same value as 1 ten, then learning that 10 tens is the same value as 1 hundred. When there are many things to count, older children also learn that it is easier and faster to skip-count by putting items into sets of twos (2, 4, 6), fives (5, 10, 15), and tens (10, 20, 30). The book makes this point as each tens number is shown in two ways: 80 feet could be 8 crabs (counting feet by 10s) or 10 spiders (counting feet by 8s).

Materials

- Markers
- Index cards

This activity works best going from whole group to small group settings. Model the activity with the whole class, but have the children work in small groups or pairs while you facilitate and scaffold their work.

Using the index cards, make several sets of counting-by-feet cards for quantities from 1 through 10 based on the book. Each card should include the numeral that represents the animal's number of feet and a drawing of the animal. Make enough sets for each child to have one card, plus a few extra ones (snails) and tens (crabs). Also create one master set that children can refer to during the activity.

Explore and Investigate Together

Ask the children what they noticed about the way different animals were combined to create numbers like three, five, and seven. Do they think a different combination of animals could be made to get the same numbers? How can six crabs and 10 insects both have 60 legs?

After several interactive read-alouds of the story, tell the children that you are going to find different ways that you can combine animals to make the same number. Explain, for example, that there is more than one way to make five, and you're going to use counting-by-feet cards to figure out how to use smaller numbers to build bigger numbers. Distribute the counting-by-feet cards at random so each child has one, and show the children the complete master set you have on display with the extra snails and crabs. Walk through the way the book creates one of the odd numbers under 10: "We know from the story that we can make five feet with a dog and a snail—the dog has four feet, and the snail has one foot. Together, that's five feet. Who thinks they are holding a card that could also be used to make five feet but

in a different way? Look at the cards on display to see which animal combinations might help you create the five feet with your card."

If the children are struggling at first, walk them through an example: "Malli, you're holding a person and a person has two feet. How many more feet do we need to make five? Three, that's right! So we could make five with one person and three snails, because each snail has one foot. Let's use the cards to check. We start with the two feet from our person, then one snail makes three feet, one more snail makes four feet, and one last snail makes five feet." Now ask if there is another way to make five.

Depending on the size of the group of children, it might be possible to put together three or more sets of cards that all show a single total. Have children announce the total number of feet and explain each part that makes up that total: "Steve and me made six with my dog card and his person card. My dog has four feet, Steve's person has two feet, and together there are six feet!"

Talk About the Math

As children use the counting-by-feet cards to build numbers, encourage them to explain their thinking out loud and to look at their cards in new ways to support flexible thinking and creative problem solving.

- Wow, Junsu, you made such a big number using only two animals! How did you figure out that a crab and a spider make 18?

- Can anyone think of another animal besides a person that has two feet?

- I'm thinking of an animal that has four feet. What kind of animal could I be thinking of? Is there another animal I could be thinking of?

Individualize the Activity

- Some children will find it helpful to focus on fewer numbers. Display fewer counting-by-feet card options (instead of going up to 10, perhaps start with cards up to 6) and start with smaller numbers.

- Extend this activity by creating and asking the children riddles, such as "A dog named Abner is standing next to his friend named Fred. Together, they have six feet. What kind of creature is Fred?" Encourage the children to talk in small groups and use their counting-by-feet cards to figure out the answer.

- For an extra challenge, invite children to make up their own riddles. Younger children might draw four legs and dictate the riddles: "Can you guess what has four legs?" Children who are confident riddle solvers can work with one or two other children to make up their own riddle. Support them in wording their riddles clearly before sharing them with another group of children to solve.

More Books

Counting Book of Bugs: Count from 1 to 13 / Cathy Cawood

Counting with Barefoot Critters / Teagan White

How Many? A Counting Book / Christopher Danielson

Other Resources

Christopher Danielson's *How Many? A Counting Book* also has a teacher's edition, which includes additional guiding questions to ask children. His blog also offers many fun, engaging ideas for families to talk to their children about math: https://talkingmathwithkids.com

COUNTING IN MY WORLD

The Routine

Nothing brings literacy to life like having children work together to make a classroom book or create one on their own. Why not add a mathematical twist?

Consider the Math Concept

Children's drawings are a window into their ideas and feelings, and providing children with opportunities to choose what they draw gives teachers a way to see objects and experiences that are meaningful to them. Children are typically very precise about who or what is depicted when it comes to identity and quantity: "There are four people in my house: me, my brother, Mama, and Grandma." Different details they choose to include might also show awareness of certain mathematical concepts, such as one-to-one correspondence: "I drew four chairs too—one for everybody!"

Many 3- and 4-year-olds and some 5-year-olds are still working on translating their ideas into a clear representation in their drawings. Encourage children to describe what they have drawn and why with open-ended questions or comments. For example, you might ask a child who has drawn three pairs of shoes, "Tell me about this picture. How did you decide to draw shoes?" When prompted to explain his thinking, the child might say, "I drew shoes for Papa Bear, Mama Bear, and Baby Bear," while pointing to each pair. His explanation and gestures to the shoes of different sizes for each character shows that he was thinking about size and comparison while he created his drawing. Have children write or dictate what they say about their work and how they made it. This is an important part of documenting their understanding of math concepts.

Materials

- Paper
- Markers and crayons
- Pencils
- Something to connect the book pages, such as staples and a stapler or a three-hole punch and brads

This activity can work as an individual, small group, or whole group activity. Determine how many pages each book will have and be sure to have enough paper. Each page will correspond to one numeral. Preschoolers can make pages for one or two numerals, which could then be compiled together into a collective class number book. Children just starting kindergarten can typically make individual books that go from 1 to 10, while children finishing up kindergarten could make individual books that go up to 20.

Explore and Investigate Together

Read a few counting books (like the ones suggested at the end of this activity) with the whole group, taking time to explore and discuss the numerals, number words, and accompanying illustrations. You might also create your own counting book to share. Ask the children what they notice about each page. Use this opportunity to help children show and count things that matter to them! For example, you might display your page for one and say: "The first page of my book is for the number 1. Here at the top, I wrote the numeral *1* nice and big. Underneath, I drew my one dog, Ferdinand. I also drew one bowl of water and one bone for Ferdinand."

Provide children with the paper, markers, crayons, and pencils, and tell them they will be making their own number books. Remind the children that their counting book will be special if it's about things that are part of their lives. As the children work on each page,

circulate around the room and talk with them about what they would like to draw, scaffolding their thinking and prompting them to make connections between things in their own life and the numbers being explored. Be sure to spend some one-on-one time with each child, asking questions and making comments that will help them be more precise in their thinking and language. Help the children label their number pages with an explanation of what is depicted. Older children can write the words to accompany their drawings, while younger children might dictate and have you write for them. Don't forget to have each child create a cover for their book too, with an illustration and a title, such as *Julia's Counting Book* or *Hugo Can Count to 10!*

Help each child or the whole class assemble their individual or collective counting books. If a class book is being made, guide the children in grouping all pages for the same number together and in the correct order (all the pages for number one go first, then all the pages for number two, etc.).

Over the next few weeks, dedicate a portion of group time to inviting the children to come up and talk about a page or two from their own book or the pages that they contributed to the class book. When the children read or talk about their books or pages to others in class, ask questions about what they've written and drawn and invite listeners to also ask questions about what they see and hear. For example, if Tanika drew three sisters on her page for the number 3, you might ask her how many of her sisters are older than her and how many are younger than her.

Put the book in the classroom library—it's very likely to be one of the most popular! You might even scan each page and share it digitally with children's families.

Talk About the Math

Here are some ideas for open-ended prompts you might use to inspire children to draw pictures that explore the concept of *how many*:

- I see you're trying to think of something for your seven page, Dean. Do you need some help brainstorming? What kinds of things do you like to play with at home?

- Think about some of the buildings in your neighborhood. Is there something you can count about them? How could you draw that?

- If you're having trouble deciding which number page to dedicate to your favorite animal, try rolling one of the die in this container. Whichever number you roll, make that the number page for your favorite animal.

Use questions and conversations to guide children to consider what they've drawn more deeply.

- Look at all the details you included in your drawing of your two pet cats, Sammy! I wonder how many legs (tails, whiskers) both cats have altogether?

- **Mr. Abbasi:** That's a lot of rainbows in your drawing. I think you must like rainbows. I do too.
  Nova: I love rainbows—I made fifteen! One rainbow for everybody in our class.
  Mr. Abbasi: And I see that some of your rainbows have two lines and some have one. How many have two lines? Did you think some friends in class would like two-line rainbows and others would like one-line rainbows?
  Nova: (*Uses her finger to count the rainbows with two lines.*) I made six rainbows with two lines. Stella told me she once saw a double rainbow so one of these is for her. She said it was a dark sky but there was a double rainbow.

Individualize the Activity

- Some children might benefit from sentence frames written on each page to help guide and focus their thinking: "I like [name of food]. Here are [number] [name of food]." Be sure the written prompts you provide leave room for children to draw the food they choose and to add to the label in their own words.

- To help children approach this activity in a more concrete way, you might ask them to pick a favorite area in the classroom space and to make drawings that show objects they see there. For example, one child might make a *Counting in the Dramatic Play Area* book, with pages like 1 stove, 2 microphones, and 3 stethoscopes.

- For an extra challenge, ask children to make pages that show the same quantity in different ways. This is something that will be helpful to model with your own counting book. For example, on the page for the number four, you might show a street with four houses in a row. Then, there could be four children, with two children next to one house and two next to another house. There could also be four birds in the picture, with three sitting on the fence and one in a nest. Ask the other children to be number detectives and see how many ways they can see a number on the page.

Related Books

Counting with / Contando con Frida / Patty Rodriguez and Ariana Stein, illus. Citlali Reyes

Found Dogs / Erica Sirotich

Stack the Cats / Susie Ghahremani

Chapter Four

MEASURING

HOW BIG IS IT?

Math Concepts Explored in this Chapter

- Attribute
- Counting
- Data
- Direct comparison

- Indirect comparison
- Magnitude
- Measurement
- Nonstandard unit of measurement

- Number operation
- Standard unit of measurement

Where's the Math?

From young to old, we often assume that *big* is good and that being bigger or having more is preferable to being smaller or having less, whether it's toys, candy, jewels, a house, or power. However, an essential part of maturing—and the main issue in many favorite children's stories— is coming to realize that saying something is *big* or *bigger* is actually a complex idea.

Exploring Measuring

Ms. Hill teaches in a mixed-age kindergarten classroom. At choice time one afternoon, she watches a group of children sorting 10 people puppets into two sets, one for each of two groups who want to act out a story they just heard. Adele, the oldest in the group at 6 years old, takes charge. She eyes the puppets everyone is holding and says, "I have the biggest. Let's see who has the smallest." One by one, she directs everyone to hand her their puppet, laying each out in a line on the floor by height.

Adele looks between the puppets that Kami and VJ, both of whom are 5 years old, are holding and asks them which of their puppets they think is taller. They're not sure until Michael suggests they hold the two puppets back to back. Once they do, they agree that VJ's is a little taller. "I think it's heavier, too," VJ explains, holding a puppet in each hand. "It feels like it's heavier." Adele adds the two puppets to the line.

When she has finished lining up the puppets, Adele pulls the five tallest puppets toward her and announces, "My group will take these. VJ, you guys can have those."

"I don't think you did it fair," Kami objects, looking at the two piles. "Me and VJ don't got as much."

"Yes, you do," Adele answers. She touches each puppet in both piles as she counts, "You've got one, two, three, four, five. We got five puppets, too. See? One, two, three, four, five!"

Kami and VJ are both quiet at this. Neither one looks convinced, but they see that Adele is right about each group having five puppets.

At this point, Ms. Hill steps in with a question. "I wonder if there's another way we can measure each puppet group to find out if one is bigger than the other. They both have the same number of puppets, but how else could we compare them?"

After studying the puppets for a few minutes, one of the children in Adele's group, Logan, suggests, "We can put them in a line like this." He begins to rearrange his group's puppets in a line, but head to feet. "And then we put theirs the same way underneath. Then we can see if the lines they make are the same long."

"That's a very helpful idea, Logan!" Ms. Hill exclaims. "By looking at the puppets this way, you can compare their length, or how long they are."

The children make quick work of lining up the puppets in this new way, and once they've finished, it's clear that the line of puppets for Adele and Logan's group is longer than the line of puppets for Kami and VJ's group.

VJ says, "See? It's the same number, but it's not really fair because you guys got the bigger five and we got the littler five!"

Adele gives a lopsided grin but doesn't object as the others rearrange the puppets into two new groups of assorted sizes.

What Kind of Bigger Is It?

Measurement is any process used to describe an attribute that can be quantified, like height, volume, and weight. When you compare objects to determine which is bigger, the comparison is made between measurable attributes that the objects share, not the objects themselves. This is why it's important to be precise in identifying which attributes are being compared, something the children in Ms. Hill's class discovered. At first, Adele used general terms like *biggest* and *smallest* to compare the puppets. As the children continued to make comparisons, they got a little more specific about types of bigness when they used labels like *taller* and *heavier*. When Adele first divided the puppets into two sets, Kami and VJ could see that Adele's group had a "bigger" set of puppets somehow, but they weren't sure how to explain why this was so. When Adele pointed out that she gave each group five puppets, she was focusing on the aspect of bigness involving number (quantity). Logan, acting on Ms. Hill's prompting, helped the others see that bigness can be measured and compared in more than one way. His suggestion to line up the puppets from each set to compare their total length sparked VJ's realization that while both sets of puppets had the same quantity, his group's were shorter (in height/length). That's how his group wasn't as "big" as Adele's.

Young children need many authentic and varied experiences to develop the higher level of abstract thinking skills needed to determine what kind of bigness is important to consider in a given situation. It is also important to give children the time and space to wrestle with questions and problems, try out some ideas, and express their thoughts to others. Ms. Hill did not immediately step in to help the children resolve their problem. When she did offer help, her scaffolding was minimal; she guided the children to reach their own resolution instead of providing them with a solution or even a process. This gave the children a chance to think through the problem more deeply.

How Can Things Be Compared?

You can compare the attributes of objects directly or indirectly. When you use your senses to compare two things—like listening to sounds to determine which is louder or lifting rocks one at a time to figure out which is heavier—you are making a *direct comparison*. In the vignette above, when the children in Ms. Hill's class lined up the people puppets and used their eyes to determine which line was longer, they were using direct comparison.

However, comparing objects' attributes using your senses alone is sometimes difficult or just not possible. For example, if children want to know which of two pumpkins is the biggest around, they might not be sure just by looking at them. In situations like this, a third object can be used to make an *indirect comparison*. The children might wind yarn around the center of each pumpkin and cut the yarn so each piece represents the circumference the pumpkin. Then, they can compare the length of the two yarn pieces to determine which is longer, and therefore which pumpkin's circumference is bigger. The comparison here is indirect because rather than comparing the objects themselves (the pumpkins) to one another, something else (yarn) is being used to represent and compare the objects.

How Much Bigger Is It?

Making a direct comparison between objects gives you information about which object is bigger in some way. For example, when VJ and Kami compared how tall their people puppets were, they were satisfied just using their eyes to make a direct comparison to determine that VJ's puppet was "a little" taller than Kami's. There are times, however, when children might want or need to know precisely how *much* bigger something is.

This is where it can be helpful to use some kind of unit of measurement to compare the specific attributes (length, weight) of objects. Children can measure and compare the attributes of objects with both nonstandard and standard units of measurement. Many ordinary items that aren't typically used to measure something, like connecting cubes (to measure a book) or your feet (to measure the length of a shelf that holds toys), can be a *nonstandard unit of measurement*. A book might be seven connecting cubes long; the shelf might be 15 of your feet long. If the children in Ms. Hill's class had wanted to figure out how much bigger VJ's puppet was than Kami's, they might have used a nonstandard unit of measurement, like paper clips, to measure the length of each puppet. This may have led to the discovery that VJ's puppet was 15 paper clips long and Kami's was 13 paper clips long. One of the children might have noted that VJ's puppet was two paper clips longer than Kami's.

As children gain experience using nonstandard units of measurement and understand how to use them to make comparisons, they'll discover that nonstandard units of measurement can change. While the shelf is 15 "feet" long when measured with *your* feet, it might be 22, 27, or 30 "feet" when children use *their* feet to measure it! You can introduce *standard units of measurement* to children by using tools that yield fixed, conventional units (inches, pounds, liters) to measure an object. Rulers, balance scales, and measuring cups are excellent standard unit tools for young children to use as they explore measurement. If the children in Ms. Hill's class had wanted to use a standard unit of measurement to compare puppets, they might have used a measuring tape and found that VJ's puppet was 12 inches long and Kami's was 10 inches long, meaning VJ's puppet was two inches longer. Counting and comparing measurable attributes in this way builds the groundwork for number operations like addition and subtraction. Keep in mind that a fuller understanding of standardized measurement typically comes when children are in the primary grades. Asking questions, experimenting, and sharing and discussing ideas are all part of the process of figuring out "how big is it?"

Making Fair Comparisons

The importance of knowing "how much bigger" is closely tied to the need to make sure a comparison is equitable, or fair. This is often of great importance to young children. They are concrete thinkers; as we saw in Ms. Hill's room, they often need evidence from a direct comparison to be sure a fair comparison is being made. However, the same attribute must be measured and compared to determine which object is bigger. When the children were comparing the groups of puppets, measuring quantity offered one type of fairness—both groups of puppets were equal in number—but measuring the size of the puppets offered a different, fairer (to the children) type of comparison. Provide young children plenty of experiences with different types of tools so they discover ways they can make more precise measurements to answer their questions. Having rich discussions around this will help them express their thoughts about whether a comparison is fair and why.

BUILDING WITH BLOCKS

Inspired by *CRASH! BOOM! A Math Tale* / Robie H. Harris, illus. Chris Chatterton

The Story

Elephant is trying to build a block tower as tall as he is. When his first attempt falls with a crash and a boom, he tries again—and again! Each time, he counts how many blocks he uses, balances them in different way, and ponders what he needs to change from last time until he finally succeeds.

Consider the Math Concept

The visuals in this book invite all kinds of rich conversations about direct comparisons. While Elephant is illustrated, the blocks he is building with are realistic photographs of the classic wooden unit blocks found in many early childhood classrooms. Realistic photos featuring materials that look and function just as they do in real life offer familiarity and support a quick transfer of ideas from the book to the children's real-life content. In other words, children read about and see something on the page that they can then manipulate, compare, and experiment with concretely for themselves.

Materials

- Unit blocks that are half unit, one unit, two units, and four units in size
- Drawings of Elephant that are 11 inches high
- Tape
- Cardboard (optional)

This activity work best in small group settings. Young children need a lot of support expressing relationships when comparing size. Be attentive to their gestures and ready to rephrase or supply vocabulary. For children whose language is still emerging, keep the group size to two or three children. This will keep engagement high when someone needs a little more time to find the words they're looking for.

Tape the drawings of Elephant to walls around the area where the children will be building their block towers. If you prefer, tape the drawings to cardboard that is cut and folded to stand on its own.

Explore and Investigate Together

Before beginning the block activity, read the book with children if they are not familiar with it. Give children the opportunity to explore and play with the blocks. Encourage them to compare the different sides or faces of the blocks, and ask if they notice any ways the blocks are the same or different. Once the children have finished this hands-on exploration, bring their attention to the illustration on the last page of the book where Elephant says "Ta-dah!" Ask them what they notice about Elephant's tower. To make his tower taller, how else did Elephant change it? How would they build a tower as tall as Elephant?

Draw attention to or bring out the drawings of Elephant, and invite the children to use the blocks to build a tower as tall as Elephant. Encourage them to experiment with using different blocks and stacking them in various ways. As the children play and talk about their discoveries, facilitate their conversations. Encourage children to continue to explore and comment on how the towers differ if they use only one size of block.

Talk About the Math

As the children build, they will realize that it doesn't work to simply talk about *bigger* or *smaller*. Instead they need to use more precise language that compares dimensions of length, such as *tall, long, short, wide, narrow, high,* and *low*. Encourage conversations about the attributes, using prompts such as these:

- Which way did you put that block, Safiyyah?
  On the narrow side or the wide side?

- Which towers seem to be sturdier? Which are wobblier?

- Is the block Tony put there longer or shorter than the one Bruce stacked?

- How many more blocks do you think your group will need to add to make your tower tall enough, Agostino? How do you know?

- This group's tower uses three blocks. That group's tower uses the same three blocks, but it is a little taller. I wonder why that is.

- Lina built a tower using four square blocks. An's tower uses only one of the tallest blocks. Both towers are as tall as Elephant, but why do you think the number of blocks is different?

Individualize the Activity

- Some children may find it challenging to build a tower, such as children with disabilities that impact their fine motor skills. Lay the drawing of Elephant flat and ask children to build a block structure that is as "long" as he is instead.

- Challenge children to build a block tower that is as tall as they are. You might guide them to use unit blocks or string to measure each other or let them determine their height and the height of the tower on their own.

- Children with a solid grasp on generalizing and thinking abstractly are ready to dig deeper into thinking about how the orientation of a block matters. Ask them to build block towers with this focus in mind, exploring the difference between piling blocks so that the narrow face is showing on top versus stacking them with the wide face showing on top. Have them document their findings with notes and drawings. You can also help them document their results by taking photographs for them to study. Have them compare the different ways they used the blocks and how the orientation and length of the blocks impacted the number of blocks they used.

More Books

Bigger! Bigger! / Leslie Patricelli

Dreaming Up: A Celebration of Building / Christy Hale

Tall / Jez Alborough

FINDING THE RIGHT FIT

Inspired by *The Three Bears* / illus. F. Rojankovsky

The Story

Goldilocks finds a house in the woods. No one is home, so she lets herself inside. She finds three bowls of porridge, three chairs, and three beds, trying each until she finds the one that is just right for her.

Consider the Math Concept

Young children tend to compare things based on themselves and their interests and needs. With a variety of experiences and conversations, over time they develop the understanding that comparisons and measurements are always relative. Exploring this concept is part of what makes this fairy tale such a meaningful and enduringly popular classic. As Goldilocks goes through the house of the three bears, the text and illustrations very clearly show that all of Papa and Mama Bear's things are not a good fit for her for one reason or another, while all of Baby Bear's are just right!

PLAN

Materials

- Cardstock or construction paper
- Markers
- Scissors

This activity works best in small group settings. It is very important that all children have a chance to express their thinking.

Explore and Investigate Together

Begin a discussion about the story with the children by asking, "Why do you think that Goldilocks always felt Baby Bear's things were just right for her?" As the children share ideas, bring up a new point: "Goldilocks said that Papa Bear's chair was too big. Do you think it was too big for Papa Bear? If you asked Papa Bear about his chair, would he say it was too big or just right for him? Why do you think that?" Help children generalize the point that measurements and comparisons are relative. In other words, what is just right for one person may not be just right for another person.

Help each child trace an outline of his foot on paper and then assist with cutting it out and labeling it with his name. This is his footprint ruler. Create a footprint ruler for yourself as well so you can model both how to make it and how to use it. Tell the children that they are going on a scavenger hunt to find objects that are the same length as their footprint rulers. Before the children begin searching the room for items, have them compare the size of their footprint rulers with each other's and talk about how they compare. Whose is shorter and whose is longer? Are they different in other ways? Ask the children how even these small differences could make something (like shoes) just right for one person but not for another.

Demonstrate measuring a few objects with your own footprint ruler, thinking aloud and inviting comments from children as you do a side-by-side comparison of something obviously much shorter or much longer, several objects that are close to the same length, and then an object that is the same length—or just right. Then have them do their own search for just-right objects.

Talk About the Math

As the children discuss their discoveries, model and encourage them to use language that describes the length of objects.

- Javier, show me how you figured out that these objects are just as long as your footprint ruler.

- Let's take a look at the objects you found, Suresh. I see a book and a unit block. Does the book seem a little longer than the block? I wonder, if the book and the block are different sizes, can they both be the same length as your footprint ruler?

- **Mrs. Gutiérrez:** What do you think about the dump truck you're holding, Natasha? Is it longer than your footprint ruler? Shorter?
  Natasha: The whole truck is too big. But this part is the same, I think. (*Gestures to the dump bed of the toy truck.*)
  Mrs. Gutiérrez: Good observation! I think you're right, but how can you tell for sure?
  Natasha: (*Holds her footprint ruler on top of the truck's dump bed.*) I was right! They're the same.
  Mrs. Gutiérrez: You were right! You found that the truck's dump bed and your footprint ruler are the same length.

Individualize the Activity

- If some children find exploring the whole space for just-right objects too overwhelming, gather just a few objects. Spread them out on a table or in a basket for the children to explore and measure against their footprint ruler.

- Because children will likely find and consider objects with a wide range of sizes and shapes, you may need to help them isolate the attribute of length. If children find it difficult to focus on just length, curate a collection of objects that have similar attributes *except* length for them to explore and measure with their footprint ruler.

- Invite children who are ready for a challenge to find and order three sets of objects: one set of objects that are shorter than their footprint ruler, one set of objects that are just right, and one set of objects that are longer. Encourage them to make drawings or help them take photos to document their discoveries and to use precise words for measuring when labeling them.

More Books

Inch by Inch / Leo Lionni

Mouse Is Small / Mary Murphy

A Pig Is Big / Douglas Florian

BIGGER THIS WAY, BIGGER THAT WAY

Inspired by *Biggest, Strongest, Fastest* / Steve Jenkins

The Story

Steve Jenkins uses his trademark realistic collages to explore big records in the animal world. As the story describes animals that are the heaviest, the strongest, and the tallest, it also drives home the message that determining which animal is biggest depends on how you define *big*.

Consider the Math Concept

This book offers many opportunities for children to think about the importance of using precise questions to determine exactly what kind of bigger is meant. For example, the first spread says that the African elephant is the biggest land animal when you look at both height *and* weight. Only a few pages later, bigness is looked at in a different way and a new animal becomes the record holder. When looking at height only, a giraffe is the biggest; it measures 19 feet high while the tallest elephant is only 13 feet high. When *all* animals on land and in the sea are considered, the blue whale is the heaviest animal; a blue whale can weigh as much as 20 elephants! Each comparison also includes a small diagram that shows an adult human or human hand next to the creature to illustrate the scale of difference.

Preschoolers can understand that there are many different measurable attributes to consider when we say something is bigger or biggest. However, children need to be in kindergarten or the early primary grades before they are able to understand that the more specific you are when defining size and other attributes, the more complex it gets. Even adults find it amazing to think that a tiny ant is the strongest animal—for its size. The accompanying diagram in the book helps show that while very strong humans can only carry something about equal to their own weight, ants can carry up to five times their own weight.

	Bigger This Way	Bigger That Way
Riddle	How is a _____ bigger than a _____?	How is a _____ bigger than a _____?
Answer	The _____ is bigger than the _____ this way: The _____ is _____.	The _____ is bigger than the _____ that way: The _____ is _____.

Materials

- Large easel, dry erase board, or chart paper
- Paper   ■ Markers

This activity works best going from whole group to small group settings. Work through a few examples with the whole class before having the children work in smaller groups where you can facilitate more closely.

For each child, create a riddle template by folding a piece of writing paper in half. On one side, create a cover template by writing the words "My Bigger This Way, Bigger That Way Riddle Is About . . . ." Leave enough space for children to write the names and draw pictures of two different animals. Inside of each folded sheet, draw a chart with column titles as shown on page 84. On the dry erase board, re-create this chart large enough for all the children to see and to allow room for multiple riddles.

Explore and Investigate Together

After you have shared the book with the children, display the first page that shows the elephant for all the children to see and ask them, "What do you remember about why the African elephant is the biggest land animal?" When they share their answers, ask questions that are more specific: "What if we look only at height? Is the African elephant the tallest? Or can someone name an animal that is taller than an elephant?" Summarize the children's comments and pose a new question for them. "Yes, that's right, everyone! We see that the giraffe is bigger than the elephant in one way—the giraffe is taller. Who can think of a way that the elephant is bigger than the giraffe?"

Work through a few more examples with all of the children by considering several measurable attributes related to the elephant, recording their responses on the chart. Reinforce each comparison by restating it: "So we said that the elephant is bigger this way because it

is *heavier* than the giraffe. But the giraffe is bigger that way because it is *taller* than the elephant."

Once the children are comfortable with how the activity works, explain that they'll have an opportunity to create their own riddles comparing two animals. In small groups, distribute the riddle templates and ask each group to choose two animals (or objects) so they can create their own Bigger This Way, Bigger That Way riddles and answers together. They can create more riddles based on the book, other stories they like, pets, furniture in the classroom, or whatever they like. At group time for the next week or so, invite different groups to present their riddles and have other children try to solve them. Use the riddles for a classroom poster or collect them in a classroom book.

Talk About the Book

Use open-ended questions and prompts to reinforce children's understanding that being specific about the kind of big makes comparisons more meaningful.

- Westley, I hear you saying that a Tyrannosaurus rex is bigger than a blue whale. What features of their size could we research and compare to see if that is true?

- What is the difference between saying something is longer and saying it is taller or higher?

- Clint and Rashid, you said a pug is bigger than a rat because it is taller, but you were stuck on finding a way that a rat is bigger than a pug. Oni, I see you're pointing to their tails. Do you think one of them has a longer tail? Which one?

Individualize the Activity

- If children find it challenging to make precise comparisons with different kinds of big, use concrete objects in the room that are significantly different in size and ask children to identify opposites: "Find something huge and put something tiny next to it." When they identify two objects to compare, help them focus on the ways one object is bigger than the other. Is it taller? Wider? Heavier? All of these things?

- Arrange three objects with dimensions of length (like height and width) that differ in several ways, such as a book, a rectangular unit block, and a ruler. Lay them out in order from longest to shortest. Then tell the children, "The ruler is first, the book is second, and the block is third. Can you figure out what kind of big I used to put these objects in this order?" Rearrange the same three items using another dimension, such as widest to narrowest.

- Challenge children whose understanding of this concept is strong to develop a more robust vocabulary to express size comparisons. Have the children help you create a word wall labeled "Better than 'Bigger' Measurement Words" showing words with more precise meanings that you and the children can use in place of the word big or bigger. To keep the word wall in use in a playful way, declare that you are going to try to go one whole day without saying big or bigger. If the children hear you using big or bigger, they can let you know and help you find a word on the wall that you could have said instead.

More Books

How Big Is Big? How Far Is Far? All Around Me / ed. Little Gestalten, illus. Jun Cen

How Big Were Dinosaurs? / Lita Judge

How Much Does a Ladybug Weigh? / Alison Limentani

THE LETTER CLUB

The Game

Names are a very important part of our identity. Playing with attributes of our names that we can measure is a powerful, engaging way to combine math and literacy.

Consider the Math Concept

There are many ways that exploring names encourages children to think about different kinds of bigness. You can measure how "big" a name is in a number of ways. For example, you might count how many letters are used to spell it. Using tally marks, connecting cubes, or some other nonstandard measuring unit to represent the number of letters helps children literally see how big a name is. You could also define and measure bigness by counting the number of syllables a name has when you say it out loud or by looking at the size of the written letters (uppercase or lowercase).

Think about ways to use these measurable attributes to compare children's names and collect data about the findings. For example, you could count and compare how many of the children's names use a specific letter or what length (number of letters) is most or least common. The great thing about this game is that the data are objective and vary for every group of people. Each will discover fun ways to look at the data!

PLAN

Materials

- Chart paper or poster board
- Index cards
- Markers, pencils, or crayons
- Connecting cubes

This activity works best in a whole group setting. Have each child write his name on an index card, helping as needed. Draw a T-chart for each letter of the alphabet on a separate piece of chart paper or poster board, labeling one column for the capital letter and the other column for the lowercase of that same letter. Leave enough space in each column to write out a list of names and to record the number of members. Display these posters around the room so everyone can see them.

Explore and Investigate Together

Ask the children to look at their name cards and the name cards of the others around them. Do they notice anything similar? Anything different? Scaffold their conversations to explore how names (typically) use both capital and lowercase letters and are made up of a different combinations of letters.

Explain that you are going to create clubs by looking at the letters in everyone's names, paying special attention to whether each letter is capital or lowercase. To measure and compare how many members are in each club, each person will use a connecting cube to create a tower that will represent how "big" the club is. You might also show them how to use tally marks to count members. Ultimately, the number of members will be measured and compared by looking at the height or length of each connecting cube tower and counted and compared using the tally marks.

Begin with a letter that is fairly common among the names of the children in your class in capital or lowercase form. Ask each child who has that letter in her name and therefore belongs to that club to write her name on the poster, make a tally mark, and contribute a cube to the club tower. Continue to call out one capital or lowercase letter at a time, inviting children to come forward to add their names to the club's list, tally count, and tower until everyone belongs to two or more clubs. You might do just a few rounds on a given day until you've gone through the whole alphabet. At the end of each day, have the children measure and compare the club towers and to count and compare the number of members using the tally marks. Study and discuss the data collected so far and how they continue to change.

Talk About the Math

Use open-ended questions and prompts to help children think more deeply about how they can measure and compare their names with others'.

- Asja, you're in the capital A club and the lowercase a club. Tell us why that is.
- Cindy and Tyvon, there are two letter clubs that both of you are in together. Do you know which ones?
- Jinsop, I noticed that you added your name to the capital P club. What do you notice about the other names in this club?

Children will also be interested in reviewing the data you have collected on the completed letter club posters. Ask them to explain what they notice as they look at the data.

- Which letter club is the biggest? Which is the smallest? Why do you think so?
- What do you notice about the how the capital I club compares with the lowercase i club, Pia?
- What would happen if we put everyone in the capital R club and the lowercase r club into one letter R club?
- Do you think our data would change if we used last names instead of first names? How?

Individualize the Activity

- If children find it challenging to identify letters for this activity, explore measurable attributes of their names in more concrete ways. Invite them to build "name towers" with connecting cubes, using one cube for each letter of their name. They can then compare the height of their name tower with other children's to see who has the "biggest" (longest) name.

- Invite children who are ready for a challenge to explore the other measurable attributes of their names, like the number of letters or syllables, and to create clubs that way.

- Children can also explore measurable attributes of words other than names. Ask them to come up with their own rules for three clubs and to write or draw pictures of members of the club. (For example, a bear and a ball might be together in the *B* club.) Have them share their categories and the rules they created with the other children.

Related Books

A, My Name Is Alice / Jane Bayer, illus. Steven Kellogg

The Construction Alphabet Book / Jerry Pallotta, illus. Rob Bolster

What If an Alligator Ate an Avalanche / Damien Macalino, illus. Eduardo Paj

Chapter Five

SPATIAL RELATIONSHIPS

WHERE IS IT?

Math Concepts Explored in this Chapter

- Compose
- Decompose
- Dimension
- Direction

- Distance
- Geometric attribute
- Geometry
- Location

- Measurement
- Perspective
- Size
- Spatial attribute

- Spatial relationship
- Spatial transformation
- Three-dimensional (3-D) shape
- Two-dimensional (2-D) shape

Children begin developing an understanding of the relationships between people, objects, and places, or *spatial relationships,* from the moment they are born. As they grow older, the question "Where is it?" comes up repeatedly in their day-to-day life, and our answers—whether it's pointing a finger or giving a verbal response like "upstairs" or "around the corner"—are full of math. Children's ability to understand and use information about position, location, direction, and shape gradually becomes more nuanced as they explore the world and have meaningful conversations with adults who help them become more precise in navigating, describing, and representing a space and manipulating the objects in it.

Exploring Spatial Relationships

Yinsen and Peter, both 4 years old, are sitting on either side of a half-finished puzzle. Peter chooses a piece and holds it up, saying, "Look, this must be part of the bridge." He tries to place it, but it doesn't quite fit. After carefully studying the picture and the way the knobs in the piece he holds swoop and dip, he rotates it in his hand and tries fitting it in the same space again. This time, it slides easily into place. Yinsen grins. "And here's the one that goes next to it," he says. "Now we have a bridge above the boat!" "Or a boat under the bridge," says Peter, laughing.

Two kindergartners in Mr. Chavez's class, Jack and Ursa, are pretending to be archaeologists. "How will we know where to dig for fossils?" asks Jack. "I know!" replies Ursa. "We need a map." Mr. Chavez watches as they gather materials

and begin to draw a map, discussing how to reach the dig site (marked with a big X) with elaborate details like crossing over a bridge that goes across the river and walking around an area of the jungle where the sneaky monkeys live. He makes a note to build on Jack and Ursa's interest in mapmaking with an activity for the whole class. He will have them create a map that shows the route they take to go from school to home each day.

Six-year-olds Margherita and Addy love playing a version of Battleship that is kept in the math learning center. "I'm aiming at B6," says Margherita. "You missed!" Addy replies. "My turn. Do you have a ship at C4?" "Nope," says Margherita. "Nobody got anywhere this round!"

While these children are all engaged in very different interactions and activities, they have something in common: they are exploring spatial relationships. Early experiences like these deepen children's understanding of where objects and people are in relation to something else and how objects fit together, and they contribute to the development of spatial relationship skills children will use every day in school and in life.

The Language of Spatial Relationships and Perspective

Young children understand the concepts related to position and location well before they have the language to express them. For example, they can see and understand that the bridge stretches *over* or *across* the river, but they might not yet have the vocabulary to describe what they see. Position words like *over, under, beneath, above, across, through, before,* and *after* are more abstract because they express the relationship *between* objects—not readily observable attributes like color or texture.

Using these terms is also a tricky concept for young children to grasp because one situation can be described with different words depending on what point of view, or *perspective,* is being considered. For example,

- Both Peter and Yinsen are right when one describes the picture their completed puzzle shows as a boat going *under* a bridge and the other describes it as a bridge *above* a boat.
- Jack is sitting to the *right* of Ursa, and Ursa is sitting to the *left* of Jack.

As you talk with children throughout the day about where people

and objects are in relationship to each other, be sure to emphasize position words. This helps them build a more robust vocabulary and develop an awareness that spatial relationships look different when viewed from different positions. Having the vocabulary to explain where an object is also helps children remember the locations of objects as well as imagine and manipulate them in their minds. For example, while at school a child can picture in her mind's eye what her dog is doing at home. She can imagine her dog sleeping on the big, squashy pillow in the corner of the living room or walking down the hall to the kitchen to drink from his water bowl by the back door. The descriptive nature of position and location language supports rich mental images of objects and actions.

Spatial Representations

Spatial relationships between objects and places can be represented with words (spoken or written), drawings, or other models that express position, movement, and direction. When Jack and Ursa were creating their map, they were making a representation of how they could reach the dig site by navigating through an imagined space. As they worked on their map, they quickly discovered that including landmarks (the bridge, the jungle) helped make their map more meaningful than if they had just drawn a curvy line showing the path that they had to follow from where they were standing to the X that marked the location of the dig site. Mr. Chavez might also have stepped in to say something like, "I wonder how far the dig site is from where you're standing. How could you explain that to someone?" A comment like this would help the children realize that the more precise they are, the easier it is for someone to follow their directions.

Eventually, they might choose to add the number of steps it would take to reach each landmark on the way to the dig site.

With plenty of hands-on opportunities to explore, describe, and represent spatial relationships, children's logical thinking and problem-solving skills become better developed. As their comprehension develops, they can begin to create and navigate even more sophisticated spatial representations. Many children are 6 or 7 years old before they can do the logical abstract reasoning that's needed to play games like Battleship, which uses a grid representation of space. To play, children must know how to name and locate points on the grid using the coordinate axes. When Margherita said she was aiming at B6, Addy had to understand how to find the right space on the grid (going to the second column, then counting down six rows) to determine if Margherita hit or missed a battleship on her board.

Spatial Transformations

Working with two-dimensional (2-D) and three-dimensional (3-D) shapes is also critical to building children's understanding of spatial relationships. As children explore the many ways they can manipulate, or *transform,* different shapes—rotating them, flipping them, cutting them in half, combining them—they are learning how shapes relate to one another and the space around them as well as how they can be constructed and deconstructed. Geoboards, pattern blocks, and jigsaw puzzles let children play with creating and fitting together 2-D shapes and discover their attributes, like how many sides (lines) a shape has, whether they're straight or curved, and how many angles there are. While playing with pattern blocks, for example, children come to see that an equilateral triangle (one that has three equal sides and three equal angles) is the basic unit of all other shapes in the set. They discover other relationships between the shapes, like how two squares can create a rectangle and two trapezoids can create a hexagon. Peter, the puzzle expert, is adept at transforming shapes to see how he can make them fit in a space. Sometimes he uses trial and error, but he has also developed strategies like intentionally rotating and flipping a puzzle piece and closely looking at its edges to consider where it can go.

As children play with 3-D objects like balls, blocks, and cans, scaffold their thinking about the defining attributes of these shapes. Beyond being able to name a ball as a *sphere* or a can as a *cylinder,* it is important for them to recognize that many 3-D shapes have faces that are made up of 2-D shapes. A pyramid, for example, has four faces that are triangles and one face that is a square. You might have children draw some 3-D objects to emphasize this point. A soccer ball looks like a circle when drawn on paper, but in real life, you know that it is 3-D and actually a sphere. As they become aware that 2-D shapes are part of 3-D shapes, children develop a deeper understanding of the ways shapes can be separated and combined to make new shapes.

Young children need to perform many types of transformations— flipping a cup upside down, rotating a toy to fit into a storage space, turning puzzle pieces—to talk about and more deeply understand spatial relationships and to learn the attributes of shapes that define them. Provide lots of high-quality experiences and discussions with rich language and observations that lead children to reason aloud, "See, it's a triangle because it has three sides!"

OBSTACLE COURSE ADVENTURES

Inspired by *Rosie's Walk* / Pat Hutchins

The Story

A hen named Rosie decides to take a walk around the farm before dinner. But look out! A hungry fox is following Rosie in hopes of having her for *his* dinner. Without being any the wiser, Rosie leads the fox through an obstacle course, one that she navigates with ease while the fox struggles to keep up.

Consider the Math Concept

This story's text is sparse (only 32 words total), but each one helps to craft a prepositional phrase that expresses movement and direction: *across the yard, through the fence, under the beehives.* As the story describes the different places Rosie goes on her walk and how she navigates each space, children love predicting how the fox will get foiled each time and seeing their predictions come to life in the illustrations—the fox ends up *in* the pond while Rosie safely walks *around* it, and he crashes *into* the beehives when Rosie simply walks *under* them.

PLAN

Materials

- A word wall with prepositions (optional)

This activity can work in small and whole group settings. Like Rosie, the children will navigate an obstacle course. Ahead of time, consider what furniture, objects, and play equipment in the indoor and outdoor learning spaces will work well as elements for the course and set them up. Think about which position words in particular you want to incorporate in the obstacle course directions.

Explore and Investigate Together

As you read the story, draw children's attention to both the position words in the text and what happens in the illustrations. Facilitate a discussion about how Rosie and the fox navigate the different places across the farm. Echo and emphasize the positional words and phrases children use. "Can anyone think of a place Rosie walks to in the farm and how she does it? That's a very good observation, Corinne. Even though the book doesn't say so, we can see that Rosie does go *down* the ramp. Great use of a position word!"

Explain that the class will be navigating their own obstacle course, just like Rosie. Give the children time to look over the space and objects that make up the obstacle course. Ask them to talk about how they think they might navigate each piece of equipment. Remind the children to focus on the position words you say as you review the path they will follow to navigate the obstacle course, like the following example: "First, we'll walk *across* the rug. Next, we'll crawl *under* the table. Then, we'll jump *over* the rope. Finally, we'll squeeze *between* the chairs." As each child moves through the obstacle course one by one, ask the children to join you in chanting the position words aloud.

Talk About the Math

Use playful questions and prompts that will help children connect the position words to the way their bodies are moving and could move through space.

- Mariana, show us how you would crawl *under* the table. Do you think you could crawl *through* the table? How about *next to* the table?
- What would you need to do with your body if I said to walk in that small space *between* the tables?
- What are some other things in the room that we could go *under*? What kind of creatures might be able to go *under* the door?
- Who wants to show us the difference between going *through* the door and going *past* the door?

Individualize the Activity

- For children who are struggling to follow the steps of the course because the language is too complex, begin with other activities that let them practice linking position words to actions—for example, games like Simon Says: "Simon says stretch your hands *above* your head. Simon says touch elbows with the person *next* to you."

- When all the children have navigated the obstacle course, work together to make a simple map that shows where Rosie went. Model how to trace her path on the map while chanting the position words; children will want to take a turn at doing the same. If you leave the map on display, many will come back to it on their own or with a friend.

- Encourage the children to come up with their own obstacle courses that the other children can try navigating later as a group. Provide paper and markers or crayons in the math and writing centers so the children can draw a map of their obstacle course or write out the directions using position words or symbols.

More Books

Bear About Town / Stella Blackstone, illus. Debbie Harter

Last Stop on Market Street / Matt de la Peña, illus. Christian Robinson

Where Are You? / Sarah Williamson

SHAPING UP A QUILT

Inspired by *Mooshka: A Quilt Story* / Julie Paschkis

The Story

Mooshka is the name of Karla's special, colorful quilt. Karla's grandmother created Mooshka with squares of fabric connected to different members of their family. Each square, or *schnitz,* holds a special memory of the family member it once belonged to. When Karla touches each schnitz, Mooshka whispers the story to her again and again, comforting her when she can't sleep. When Karla's baby sister is born, Karla must learn the importance of sharing Mooshka and the joyful memories and wisdom of their ancestors it holds.

Consider the Math Concept

Making patchwork quilts is a craft seen across time and cultures. At its core, it's about joining small pieces of fabric into larger units or blocks that are then joined together as a bed covering. Colorful quilt pieces and patterns frame nearly every page of Paschkis's book. They include colors, shapes, and images that all children will delight in seeing and investigating!

Looking at the quilt-work in this book (along with any additional pictures of quilts or real quilts you can bring in for the children to study) can lead to rich discussions with children about shapes and how they fit together. It's also an opportunity to identify and name shapes and define and classify their attributes (like number of lines and angles).

Investigating quilts also invites children to explore the ways smaller shapes can be composed and decomposed, fit together, and manipulated (like being flipped and rotated) to create a larger whole. Traditional quilt patterns tend to use geometric shapes such as triangles and rectangles of different sizes. When you look closely at the illustrations of Mooshka, you can see how a triangle is the basic unit shape in the quilt. Contrast these blocks with the borders on several pages that feature quilt blocks that are made up of trapezoids and rectangles.

Materials

- Cardboard or foam sheets
- Patterned and solid cardstock, construction paper, or pattern blocks
- Scissors
- Markers
- Baskets or boxes
- Laminating sheets (optional)
- Nontoxic glue (optional)

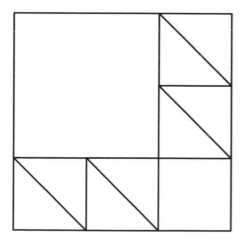

This activity works best in small group settings. Work with groups of no more than four children so they can easily share a quilt block board and see and refer to each other's work.

Cut the cardboard or foam sheets into squares (approximately 12" × 12" or similar). Choose a pattern made up of several different shapes, and draw or trace it on each cardboard square to create quilt block boards. You could create your own design or look up a pattern in a quilting book or online. The Bear Paw pattern (seen on this page) is a great choice that features different size squares and right triangles (triangles with a 90° angle).

Using cardstock or construction paper, cut out shapes to correspond with the design you've drawn on the quilt block boards. Alternately, you might have the children use pattern blocks. Prepare a basket for each small group and include enough shape cutouts in it for the group to complete one quilt block board. For durability, you might laminate the shape cutouts. If you feel that the children in your class are ready to work on individual, smaller quilt block boards (approximately 6" × 6"), create and provide enough materials accordingly.

Explore and Investigate Together

Study the illustrations in the book (including the endpapers) with the children. Ask them what details they notice in Mooshka. "What shapes do you see in Karla's blanket? Do you see a specific way those shapes might be arranged?" Be sure that children see different examples of the same shape, so you can talk about defining attributes. "We discovered that Karla's quilt is made up of many triangles. How are these triangles the same, and how are they different? What are some things you notice about triangles? How are the triangles in this quilt arranged? How can we use triangles to make other shapes? Do you see an example of triangles making another shape when you look at Mooshka?" This study of quilt shapes and how those smaller shapes are arranged to create larger ones can be extended by looking at pictures of other quilts and, if possible, real quilts.

Tell the children that they will be working together to create their own quilt block. Give each group a quilt block board and a basket of shape cutouts. Explain that each person in the group will take turns selecting a shape cutout from the basket and together they'll determine where it fits on their quilt block board. Emphasize that because smaller shapes make up bigger shapes, there could be different ways to complete their quilt block board.

Once finished, you might help the children glue down the shape cutouts to their quilt block boards and arrange and glue the quilt block boards together onto a larger sheet of cardboard or poster board, showing them how each square makes up part of the special class quilt!

Talk About the Math

As the children consider different shapes and where they can fit on their quilt block boards, prompt them to look at shapes from different angles and orientations.

- Raphael, you noticed that there's a space on the quilt block board in the shape of a square. Do you think you can make a square using other shapes? What shapes could you use?

- I wonder if you could turn that shape another way so it will fit in that space on the quilt block board, Sabrina.

Model and encourage children to use words that describe attributes of the shapes, such as *side, edge, corner, point, angle, straight, big,* and *small*. Talk about general location of the shapes and where they are in relation to other shapes:

- What shape is that in the top corner of the quilt block board, above the small triangle?

- That's such a wonderful observation, Danny! You were able to put the big square on the bottom edge of your quilt block board, but Arin found a place in the middle of his quilt block board where the big square could fit.

- I see a triangle here on Song's quilt block board with the point facing up. Can anyone find a triangle on their quilt block board with the point facing a different direction?

Individualize the Activity

- If some children struggle with this activity, have them explore composing and decomposing shapes without the framework of a quilt block board. For example, ask them to find out how many ways they can make a hexagon using other shapes. Alternately, create a simpler version of the quilt block board that features a pattern with no more than six to eight pieces.

- Ask children who are ready for a challenge to close their eyes and choose a shape cutout from their basket. See if they can guess what shape they are holding without looking by feeling its features, like the points and edges.

- Some children might see stars, flowers, or other designs in the shapes on their boards. Encourage them to tell a story about what they see, helping them make connections between shapes, objects, and experiences in their lives.

More Books

The Josefina Story Quilt / Eleanor Coerr, illus. Bruce Degen

The Patchwork Path: A Quilt Map to Freedom / Bettye Stroud, illus. Erin Susanne Bennett

The Quiltmaker's Gift / Jeff Brumbeau, illus. Gail de Marcken

SHAPE SCAVENGER HUNT

Inspired by *City Shapes* / Diana Murray, illus. Bryan Collier

The Story

Discover how shapes are hiding in plain sight everywhere you look as the girl in this book explores her city and talks about the many shapes that she finds.

Consider the Math Concept

Both the rhyming text and artwork composed of multimedia collages in this book call attention to the many 2-D shapes that can be found in bustling city spaces: rectangles in street signs, squares in windows, diamonds in kites, and so much more.

In the real world, these shapes are faces of 3-D objects. The bubbles the girl sees are actually spheres, the circles at the end of the kaleidoscope and at the top of a trashcan are one face of a cylinder, and the buildings are cubes and rectangular prisms.

PLAN

Materials

- Large easel, dry erase board, or chart paper
- Markers
- Clipboards with paper
- Pencils
- Geometric shape blocks

This activity works best going from whole group to small group settings. Work through a few examples with the whole class before having the children gather in smaller groups that you can facilitate more closely.

Explore and Investigate Together

While slowly paging through the book, invite the children to identify the examples of the 2-D shapes that the girl sees. Have them study the illustrations on one of the pages more closely, such as the spread that features a truck, a food cart, and packages. Bring out geometric shape blocks and ask which is closest to being like the shapes you see when looking at a real truck or box: "The girl calls them squares, and she's right that you can see a square when you look at just one side of a truck or a box. But let's think about all the sides of a box. Which of these blocks looks like a box you've seen in real life?" Scaffold a discussion about how the faces of a 3-D shape are 2-D shapes. A truck, for example, might have two square faces and four rectangular ones. Do the same kind of analysis and discussion for other shapes featured in the book. Have the children look at and hold the geometric shape blocks and describe their attributes: "Excellent observation, Ze'ev. The cylinder has two faces that are circles and one curved side. It's a continuous curved side."

Work with the children to make lists of objects that get described as squares, rectangles, triangles, circles, and ovals in the book. Write their responses on the dry erase board. Then, have the children work with a partner or a small group to go on a scavenger hunt to find 3-D objects in the classroom that have at least one face that is the same as one of the 2-D shapes explored in the book. Have them record their findings on their clipboards, assisting as needed. If possible, have them bring the object with them to talk about it when everyone comes together at the end of the activity to discuss their findings.

Talk About the Math

Get children thinking more deeply about the attributes of both 2-D and 3-D shapes.

- Kamir, you found a really unique object with a circular face. That was a very good point you made when you said that because the ice cream cone from the dramatic play area has only one circular face, it is not a cylinder. You're right, a cylinder needs two circular faces, one on each end.

- So many of you found items with square and rectangular faces! Does anyone have any ideas about why those shapes are so common?

- Dexter, your group labeled this long storage box underneath the chalkboard as a cube. Let's take a closer look. You were right when you said some of the faces are squares, but what shape or shapes are the other faces? If all of the faces aren't squares, do you think it's still a cube?

- How many faces can we see on a closed door? How about when the door is open? Let's try to describe how the faces are the same and different.

Individualize the Activity

- For children whose understanding of the relationship between 2-D and 3-D shapes is still developing, give them additional time to explore the geometric shape blocks. Provide a limited selection of 3-D objects for them to study for 2-D face shapes. Encourage them to feel the edges and trace each shape with their fingers to get them familiar with the features.

- If children are stuck while on their scavenger hunt, offer some clues to help them along: "I see an object by Gaëlle's feet that would look like a circle if I drew a picture of it, but in real life, it's curved all the way around."

- Strengthen the home–school connection by sending home a list of 3-D shapes illustrated with pictures of common household items that are that shape. Ask families to help their children find and label different examples of real-life objects that are those shapes.

More Books

Crescent Moons and Pointed Minarets: A Muslim Book of Shapes / Hena Khan, illus. Mehrdokht Amini

Shapes, Reshape! / Silvia Borando

Which One Doesn't Belong? A Shapes Book / Christopher Danielson

BUILD-IT CHALLENGE

The Game

Playing with building materials is a powerful way to develop spatial reasoning and problem-solving skills. While children play with blocks and other building materials on their own and make discoveries independently, offering them a challenge and discussing their unique solutions can get them thinking and talking about math at a deeper level.

Consider the Math Concept

Challenges that ask children to find their own solutions to a task with certain restrictions are somewhere between puzzles and games. There is no right or wrong solution, so children are motivated to make thoughtful choices, sketch plans to guide their thinking and building, and be comfortable using a lot of trial and error to meet the challenge. Deep learning comes from conversations you have with the children about how they used their understanding of the attributes of the materials to successfully meet the conditions of the building challenge.

PLAN

Materials

- Various building materials like unit blocks, magnetic building tiles, and boxes
- Poster board
- Markers
- Graph paper
- Pencils
- Camera

This activity works best in a small group setting so you can observe, document, and facilitate (as needed) the children's processes of planning, building, and sharing their creations.

Create a poster that clearly states the requirements for the building challenge, or create challenge cards for each group. Show a sketch and the name of different structures for children to build; decide if you should build in some requirements.

Create a Build-It Challenge center with a sign-up sheet where children write their names and what they are building. The space should also include the poster or challenge cards.

Explore and Investigate Together

Go over the challenge with the whole group: children will work together with one or two partners to create a structure listed on the poster (or the challenge cards). Have each group choose what they are going to build as well as up to 20 pieces of building materials. Let children pick their partners to work with. Announce that the challenge will continue over a week and everyone will have a chance to create a structure.

Before they begin to build, ask the children to sketch plans for their structure. What will it look like from the side or the top? As children work on the challenge, talk about the different ways a block can be oriented. For example, the long rectangular block can be stood on the smaller face to make a taller structure; but placing the larger face flat can make the tower more stable. Take photos to document their work.

Ask the children to draw their structures again after they have finished. This will help them better understand how a construction looks different depending on the side they are looking at or whether they are viewing it from the top down. Explore how the building looks different from and the same as the drawings they made before they started building. Have each team take a photo of their completed tower that gets posted along with a sketch of their plans, a drawing of the finished structure, and a building report that identifies which blocks they used. (Consider giving children a template to complete.)

Bring the project to a close by developing and discussing a data chart:

- Which shape and size blocks were used most often?
- Were there any blocks that no one chose?
- How much difference was there in the height of the "high" towers?
- What were differences in the design of sturdy versus high towers?

Compile the documentation, the building reports, and the final data chart together in a notebook to keep near the block area. Encourage children to try to reproduce someone else's design or to make a new one, which can be added to the book.

Talk About the Math

While it's important that children do their own problem solving, carefully observe them as they work and ask guiding questions that will encourage them to experiment and take risks and that will support children who seem to be stuck or frustrated.

- Akio, it looks like you and Tommy are trying to stack all of your blocks on their shortest edge so you can make the tallest tower, but your tower keeps tumbling down. Is there another way you could stack some of the blocks to make your tower sturdier?
- Your group combined cardboard boxes and magnetic tiles to make your tower, Xio. Tell me more about why you decided to use these building materials.
- Ali, as soon as you picked up the pyramid block I heard you say that it was going to be the roof for your tower. What made you decide that?
- The drawings you made of your tower before and after building it are so detailed, Seb. Can you explain them to me? Is this one showing me the tower from the top or from the side? Does your tower actually look like this when you look at it from that angle?

FINAL THOUGHTS

We hope this book has sparked excitement about the many ways you can use stories, games, and routines to awaken and extend children's wonderings about math. Mathematical thinking and problem solving are dynamic processes, which is what makes playing with the math so engaging for everyone. The suggestions and ideas in this book are not meant to be considered a step-by-step guide. Instead, think of each activity as a starting point that you can tailor and rework to meet the needs and interests of the children you teach. Don't feel limited to the books or games we've suggested in these pages. In fact, we are always finding new books to share with children, and every time we engage children in one of the experiences in this book, we tweak it.

If there's one thing we'd like you to take away from this book, it's this: *math is everywhere*. It will take some thinking, but you have the skills and ingenuity to take stories and games that strike a chord for the children you work with and mathematize them. Remember that some of the very best ideas and new directions for exploration and learning come from children's own stimulating questions and thoughts. Listen to the questions children ask you, each other, and themselves every day, and show them how math can help them discover the answers they're looking for.

GLOSSARY

abstraction: the principle related to counting that states that any set of objects that can be seen, touched, heard, or imagined can be counted, whether it is made up of objects that are similar to or completely different from one another

attribute: a quality, characteristic, or property that describes someone or something (for example, color, shape, size, texture, or number)

binary sorting: sorting a collection of objects into two mutually exclusive sets or groups, one with a specific attribute and one without that specific attribute

cardinality: the understanding that, when counting objects, the last number word represents the total quantity of objects in the set

comparing: observing and analyzing similarities and differences between objects

comparing and ordering sets: observing and analyzing similarities and differences between sets of objects (especially when using specifically mathematical attributes such as quantity or magnitude), then organizing or ranking those sets according to their attributes

compose: to combine parts or subsets to form a larger whole, such as with quantity or shapes

copying patterns: duplicating the structural sequence of a pattern

counting: see *rational counting* and *rote counting*

creating patterns: establishing a rule to arrange a collection of objects, events, or attributes in a sequence that follows a recognizable and predictable order or progression

data: information that can be collected, compared, analyzed, and interpreted to draw a conclusion that answers a question

decompose: to break apart or separate a whole into smaller parts or subsets, such as with quantity or shapes

dimension: in measurement, a specific attribute, such as height, width, depth, or capacity

direct comparison: using your senses to compare objects' observable attributes

exact matching: creating a set of objects that have all the same attributes

extending patterns: showing or predicting what comes next in a pattern; elements can be added either to the beginning or end of a pattern's sequence to continue it

geometric attribute: mathematical attributes of shapes, including number and length of sides (lines) and number and size of angles

geometry: the study of spatial relationships and shapes

growing pattern: sequences where the pattern is added to (increased) or taken away from (decreased) in a consistent, predictable size or amount

indirect comparison: using units or tools to represent, measure, and compare objects' attributes

logical-mathematical thinking: using mathematical reasoning skills to identify and analyze a problem to find a solution

magnitude: the relative size or amount of an object or set, determined through comparison

mathematize: to use mathematical language and concepts to frame, analyze, and explore information and situations in daily life

measurement: any process used to describe an attribute that can be quantified, like height, volume, and weight

multiple set sorting: using one or more attributes to sort one set of objects into more, increasingly complex sets

nonstandard unit of measurement: any ordinary item that isn't typically used to measure something and that yields measurements that vary depending on the particular tool used

number operation: a mathematical process, such as addition and subtraction, used to answer "how much" or "how many"

number sense: the ability to understand how many items are in a set and how to use number words to convey that quantity; to compare and see relationships between different quantities; and to be flexible with numbers when calculating and problem solving

number words: the words or names we say, think, or write to represent numbers when counting (*three, four, five*)

object order irrelevance: the principle related to counting that states that no matter how objects in a group are arranged or what order they are counted in, the quantity of objects will not change

one-to-one correspondence: the principle related to counting that states that only one number word is named for each object being counted

open sort: a flexible sorting task where the person doing the sorting identifies and describes what attributes will be used to create categories and sort a collection of objects into sets

pattern: a sequence in which several objects, events, or attributes follow a recognizable order or progression in a predictable way

perspective: the point of view being considered when exploring and describing spatial relationships

quantity: the attribute of a set of objects that indicates the number of objects

rational counting: accurately attaching a number word to items in a collection to indicate how many of something there is

recognizing patterns: being aware of and identifying regularity and sequence

repeating pattern: a sequence that contains elements that predictably and continuously repeat

rote counting: memorizing and reciting number words in the right order

set: any collection of things that is grouped together in a meaningful way

single attribute sorting: using matching skills to create sets from a collection of objects by considering just one attribute, such as color or shape

size: how big or small someone or something is according to different measurable attributes like length, area, or volume

spatial attribute: a characteristic or property that describes shape, orientation, location, direction, or relative position in space

spatial relationship: how an object is located in space in relation to another object

spatial transformation: manipulating objects like shapes by rotating them, flipping them, cutting them in half, or combining them to understand how they relate to each other and the space around them

stable order: the principle related to counting that states that number words must be said in the same sequence every time because they have a fixed meaning as a growing pattern

standard unit of measurement: fixed, conventional units (inches, pounds, liters) to measure an object, yielded by standard unit tools like rulers, balance scales, and measuring cups

structure: the way in which various elements in a pattern are organized and related

subitize: to see a small number of objects and be able to tell how many there are without counting them

three-dimensional (3-D) shape: a solid shape that has three measurable attributes, such as length, width, and height, to create depth

translating patterns: using new materials or ways to represent a pattern's structure

two-dimensional (2-D) shape: a flat shape that has two measurable attributes, such as length and width

BOOK LIST

A, My Name Is Alice. 1992. J. Bayer. Illus.
S. Kellogg. New York: Puffin Books.

Baby Goes to Market. 2017. Atinuke. Illus. A.
Brooksbank. Somerville, MA: Candlewick.

Baby Shark. 2018. J.J. Bajet.
New York: Scholastic.

Bear About Town. 2000. S. Blackstone.
Illus. D. Harter. Cambridge,
MA: Barefoot Books.

Bigger! Bigger! 2018. L. Patricelli.
Somerville, MA: Candlewick.

Biggest, Strongest, Fastest. 1997. S.
Jenkins. Boston, MA: HMH Books.

*Billions of Bricks: A Counting Book
About Building*. 2016. K. Cyrus.
New York: Henry Holt.

Bread, Bread, Bread. 1993. A. Morris. Illus.
K. Heyman. New York: HarperCollins.

*Brown Bear, Brown Bear, What Do
You See?* 1996. B. Martin, Jr. Illus.
E. Carle. New York: Henry Holt.

City Shapes. 2016. D. Murray.
Illus. B. Collier. New York: Little,
Brown and Company.

Come On, Rain! 1999. K. Hesse. Illus.
J.J. Muth. New York: Scholastic.

The Construction Alphabet Book.
2006. J. Pallotta. Illus. R. Bolster.
Watertown, MA: Charlesbridge.

Counting Book of Bugs: Count from 1 to 13.
2016. C. Cawood. Tokyo: Cathleen Cawood.

Counting with Barefoot Critters. 2016. T.
White. Toronto, ON: Tundra Books.

Counting with/Contando con Frida.
Bilingual ed. 2018. P. Rodriguez & A. Stein.
Illus. C. Reyes. Los Angeles: Lil' Libros.

CRASH! BOOM! A Math Tale. 2018.
R.H. Harris. Illus. C. Chatterton.
Somerville, MA: Candlewick.

*Crescent Moons and Pointed Minarets:
A Muslim Book of Shapes*. 2018.
H. Khan. Illus. M. Amini. San
Francisco: Chronicle Books.

Down by the Barn. 2014. W.
Hillenbrand. New York: Two Lions.

Dreaming Up: A Celebration of Building.
1996. C. Hale. New York: Lee & Low Books.

Five Creatures. 2005. E. Jenkins. Illus.
T. Bogacki. New York: Square Fish.

*Five Green and Speckled Frogs: A
Count-and-Sing Book*. 2016. P.
Burris. New York: Scholastic.

Found Dogs. 2017. E. Sirotich. New
York: Dial Books for Young Readers.

Goodbye Summer, Hello Autumn. 2016.
K. Pak. New York: Henry Holt.

Grandma's Tiny House: A Counting Story!
2017. J. Brown-Wood. Illus. P. Burris.
Watertown, MA: Charlesbridge.

The Growing Story. 2007. R. Krauss. Illus.
H. Oxenbury. New York: HarperCollins.

Head, Shoulders, Knees and Toes . . . 2002.
Illus. A. Kubler. Auburn, ME: Child's Play.

Home. 2015. C. Ellis. Somerville,
MA: Candlewick.

*How Big Is Big? How Far Is Far? All Around
Me*. 2018. Ed. Little Gestalten. Illus.
Jun Cen. New York: Little Gestalten.

How Big Were Dinosaurs? 2013. L.
Judge. New York: Roaring Brook.

How Many? A Counting Book. 2018. C.
Danielson. Portsmouth, NH: Stenhouse.

How Many Jelly Beans? 2012.
A. Menotti. Illus. Y. Labat. San
Francisco: Chronicle Books.

How Much Does a Ladybug Weigh? 2016.
A. Limentani. New York: Boxer Books.

I'm a Little Teapot! 2007. Illus. A.
Kubler. Auburn, ME: Child's Play.

Inch by Inch. 2018. L. Lionni. New
York: Dragonfly Books.

Is Your Mama a Llama? 1997. D. Guarino.
Illus. S. Kellogg. New York: Scholastic.

The Josefina Story Quilt. 2003. E. Coerr.
Illus. B. Degen. New York: HarperCollins.

Last Stop on Market Street. 2015.
M. Peña. Illus. C. Robinson. New
York: G.P. Putnam's Sons.

*Look at That Building! A First Book
of Structures*. 2011. S. Ritchie.
Toronto, ON: Kids Can Press.

"A Lost Button." In *Frog and Toad Are Friends*. 2003. A. Lobel. New York: HarperCollins.

The Mitten. 2009. J. Brett. New York: G.P. Putnam's Sons.

Mooshka: A Quilt Story. 2012. J. Paschkis. Atlanta, GA: Peachtree.

A Mother for Choco. 1996. K. Kasza. New York: Puffin Books.

Mouse Is Small. 2017. M. Murphy. Somerville, MA: Candlewick.

The Napping House. 2009. A. Wood. Illus. D. Wood. Boston, MA: HMH Books.

One Duck Stuck: A Mucky Ducky Counting Book. 2003. P. Root. Illus. J. Chapman. Somerville, MA: Candlewick.

One Is a Snail, Ten Is a Crab: A Counting by Feet Book. 2010. A.P. Sayre & J. Sayre. Illus. R. Cecil. Somerville, MA: Candlewick.

Over in a River: Flowing Out to the Sea. 2013. M. Berkes. Illus. J. Dubin. Nevada City, CA: Dawn Publications.

The Patchwork Path: A Quilt Map to Freedom. 2007. B. Stroud. Illus. E.S. Bennett. Somerville, MA: Candlewick.

Pete the Cat: I Love My White Shoes. 2010. E. Litwin. Illus. J. Dean. New York: HarperCollins.

A Pig Is Big. 2000. D. Florian. New York: Greenwillow Books.

Plant the Tiny Seed. 2017. C. Matheson. New York: HarperCollins.

The Pout-Pout Fish. 2008. D. Diesen. Illus. D. Hanna. New York: Farrar, Straus and Giroux.

Pumpkin Pumpkin. 1990. J. Titherington. New York: Greenwillow Books.

The Quiltmaker's Gift. 2001. J. Brumbeau. Illus. G. Marcken. New York: Scholastic.

Rosie's Walk. 1971. P. Hutchins. New York: Aladdin.

Sam Sorts. 2017. M. Jocelyn. Toronto, ON: Tundra Books.

Same, Same but Different. 2011. J.S. Kostecki-Shaw. New York: Henry Holt.

Shapes, Reshape! 2016. S. Borando. Somerville, MA: Candlewick.

Shoes, Shoes, Shoes. 1995. A. Morris. New York: Lothrop, Lee & Shepard Books.

Six Dots: A Story of Young Louis Braille. 2016. J. Bryant. Illus. B. Kulikov. New York: Alfred A. Knopf.

Sort It Out! 2008. B. Mariconda. Illus. S. Rogers. Mount Pleasant, SC: Arbordale.

Sorting at the Market. 2011. T. Steffora. Chicago: Heinemann-Raintree.

Soup Day. 2010. M. Iwai. New York: Henry Holt.

Stack the Cats. 2017. S. Ghahremani. New York: Abrams Appleseed.

Sun. 2017. S. Usher. London: Templar.

Tall. 2006. J. Alborough. London: Walker Books.

The Three Bears. 2012. Illus. F. Rojankovsky. New York: Golden Books.

Types of Precipitation. 2018. N. Higgins, illus. Sara Infante. North Mankato, MN: Cantato Learning.

Un Elefante: Numbers/Números. Bilingual ed. 2018. P. Rodriguez & A. Stein. Illus. C. Reyes. Los Angeles: Lil' Libros.

The Water Hole. 2004. G. Base. New York: Puffin Books.

What If an Alligator Ate an Avalanche. 2013. D. Macalino. Illus. E. Paj. Hillsboro, OR: Crystal Mosaic Books.

What We Wear: Dressing Up Around the World. 2012. M. Ajmera, E.H. Derstine, & C. Pon. Watertown, MA: Charlesbridge.

When I Build with Blocks. 2012. N. Alling. Scotts Valley, CA: CreateSpace.

Where Are You? 2017. S. Williamson. New York: Alfred A. Knopf.

Which One Doesn't Belong? A Shapes Book. 2016. C. Danielson. Portsmouth, NH: Stenhouse.

REFERENCES

Antell, S.E., & D.P. Keating. 1983. "Perception of Numerical Invariance in Neonates." *Child Development* 54 (3): 695–701.

Clements, D., & J. Sarama. 2010. "Learning Trajectories in Early Mathematics – Sequences of Acquisition and Teaching." In *Encyclopedia on Early Childhood Development: Numeracy,* e1–e8. QC, Canada: Centre of Excellence for Early Childhood Development & Strategic Knowledge Cluster on Early Child Development.

Early Math Collaborative (Early Math Collaborative at Erikson Institute). 2014. *Big Ideas of Early Mathematics: What Teachers of Young Children Need to Know.* Upper Saddle River, NJ: Pearson Education.

Gopnik, A., A.N. Meltzoff, & P.K. Kuhl. 2001. *The Scientist in the Crib: What Early Learning Tells Us About the Mind.* New York: Perennial.

NGA (National Governors Association Center for Best Practices) & CCSSO (Council of Chief State School Officers). 2010. *Common Core State Standards for Mathematics.* Washington, DC: NGA & CCSSO. www.ccsso.org/sites /default/files/2017-12/ADA%20 Compliant%20Math%20Standards.pdf.

Rasmussen, C., E. Ho, E. Nicoladis, J. Leung, & J. Bisanz. 2006. "Is the Chinese Number-Naming System Transparent? Evidence from Chinese-English Bilingual Children." *Canadian Journal of Experimental Psychology* 60 (1): 60–67.

Sarnecka, B.W. 2016. "How Numbers Are Like the Earth (and Unlike Faces, Loitering, or Knitting)." In *Core Knowledge and Conceptual Change,* eds. D. Barner & A.S. Baron, 151–170. New York: Oxford University Press.

RESOURCES

Church, E.B. n.d. "The Math in Music and Movement." *Scholastic*. Accessed April 9, 2019. www.scholastic.com/teachers/articles/teaching-content/math-music-movement.

Davis, S. 2018. "Baking Math for Families and Young Children." *NAEYC* (blog). July 6. www.naeyc.org/resources/blog/baking-math.

Dombrink-Green, M., & H. Bohart, eds. With K.N. Nemeth. 2015. *Spotlight on Young Children: Supporting Dual Language Learners*. Washington, DC: NAEYC.

Geist, E. n.d. "Support Math Readiness Through Music." *NAEYC*. Accessed April 9, 2019. www.naeyc.org/our-work/families/support-math-readiness-through-music.

Ginsburg, H. 2017. "What Young Children Know and Need to Learn About Pattern and Algebraic Thinking." Stanford, CA: Development and Research in Early Math Education. http://prek-math-te.stanford.edu/system/files/media/documents/2017/what_children_know_and_need_to_know_about_pattern_and_algebra_expanded_version.pdf.

Goldenberg, E.P., & D.H. Clements. 2014. *Developing Essential Understanding of Geometry and Measurement for Teaching Mathematics in Pre-K–Grade 2*. Reston, VA: National Council of Teachers of Mathematics.

Heroman, C. 2016. *Making and Tinkering with STEM: Solving Design Challenges with Young Children*. Washington, DC: NAEYC.

McCray, J.S., J.-Q. Chen, & J.E. Sorkin, eds. 2019. *Growing Mathematical Minds: Conversations Between Developmental Psychologists and Early Childhood Teachers*. New York: Routledge.

Moomaw, S. 2011. *Teaching Mathematics in Early Childhood*. Baltimore: Brookes.

Platas, L.M. 2018. "Measuring Up! Measurement in the Preschool Classroom." *Development and Research in Early Math Education Blog*. March 14. https://dreme.stanford.edu/news/measuring-measurement-preschool-classroom.

Platas, L.M. n.d. "The Mathematics of Geometry and Spatial Relations." *DREME TE*. Accessed April 9, 2019. http://prek-math-te.stanford.edu/spatial-relations/mathematics-geometry-and-spatial-relations.

Rosales, A.C. 2015. *Mathematizing: An Emergent Math Curriculum Approach for Young Children*. St. Paul, MN: Redleaf.

Strasser, J., & L.M. Bresson. 2017. *Big Questions for Young Minds: Extending Children's Thinking*. Washington, DC: NAEYC.

ACKNOWLEDGMENTS

This book owes much to our longtime thought partners at Erikson Institute's Early Math Collaborative, especially Jie-Qi Chen, Lisa Ginet, Jennifer McCray, Jeanine Brownell, Donna Johnson, Rebeca Itzkowich, and Cody Meirick, as well as the Collaborative's gifted coaches and staff.

We also extend our heartfelt gratitude to the many outstanding teachers, administrators, librarians, families, and researchers we've had the pleasure of working with—you have inspired us and influenced our work in so many important ways.

At the end of the day, we could never have written this book without the input of the legion of wonderful children with whom we have shared questions and conversations about the math in books and stories over many years. Understandably, we are especially grateful to those we are closest to: Mary's four sons and seven granddaughters and Laura's daughter, Julie, and her cousins. It goes without saying that we owe a great deal to our lifelong learning partners, Gordon Berry and William Thompson, for the hours of listening, asking open-ended questions, and feeding our passion for finding math all around us.

ABOUT THE AUTHORS

Mary Hynes-Berry, PhD, has more than 40 years of experience teaching through oral storytelling while working directly with young children. Her original focus was literacy, but she soon began to find ways to weave in mathematics as she worked with preservice and in-service early childhood professionals. Mary is a faculty member at Erikson Institute in Chicago and a founding member of Erikson Institute's Early Math Collaborative, which provides professional development and carries out applied research on foundational math in early childhood. She is the author of *Don't Leave the Story in the Book: Using Literature to Guide Inquiry in Early Childhood Classrooms* (Teachers College Press, 2012) and a contributing author of *Big Ideas of Early Mathematics: What Teachers of Young Children Need to Know* (Pearson, 2014) and *Growing Mathematical Minds: Conversations Between Developmental Psychologists and Early Childhood Teachers* (Routledge, 2019).

Laura Grandau, PhD, has worked in STEM education for 25 years in schools, museums, libraries, and nature centers, emphasizing curiosity and play as central components of learning. She is adjunct faculty at Erikson Institute as well as a teacher educator, researcher, and classroom teacher with expertise in teaching and learning math and science. Formerly, she served as manager of education programs at the Museum of Science and Industry, Chicago and senior program developer for Erikson Institute's Early Math Collaborative. Laura has worked extensively coaching preservice and in-service teachers and supporting curriculum and instructional planning with school leadership teams. She is a contributing author of *Growing Mathematical Minds: Conversations Between Developmental Psychologists and Early Childhood Teachers* (Routledge, 2019), and her work has also been published in numerous journals, including *Teaching Children Mathematics, Cognition and Instruction,* and *Harvard Educational Review.*

NAEYC's Bestselling Books

Great Books for Preschool and
Kindergarten Teachers

Order online at
NAEYC.org/shop
or 1-800-424-2460

Item 1130 • 2017 • 144 pages

Explore science, technology, engineering, and math (STEM) concepts through making and tinkering! With 25 classroom-ready engineering design challenges inspired by children's favorite books, educators can seamlessly integrate making and tinkering and STEM concepts in preschool through third grade classrooms. Challenge children to use everyday materials and STEM concepts to design and build solutions to problems faced by characters in their favorite books. This practical, hands-on resource includes

› 25 engineering design challenges appropriate for children ages 3–8

› Suggestions for creating a makerspace environment for children

› A list of 100 picture books that encourage STEM-rich exploration and learning

› Questions and ideas for expanding children's understanding of STEM concepts

Item 1132 • 2017 • 160 pages

Questions are powerful tools, especially in the classroom. Asking rich, thoughtful questions can spark young children's natural curiosity and illuminate a whole new world of possibility and insight. But what are "big" questions, and how do they encourage children to think deeply? With this intentional approach—rooted in Bloom's Taxonomy—teachers working with children ages 3 through 6 will discover how to meet children at their individual developmental levels and stretch their thinking. With the guidance in this book as a cornerstone in your day-to-day teaching practices, learn how to be more intentional in your teaching, scaffold children's learning, and promote deeper understanding.